Footprint Handbook

Bilbao &
Basque Region

ANDY SYMINGTON

This is
Bilbao &
Basque
Region

Europe's oldest people are in many ways Spain's most modern, always a step ahead of the rest in social attitudes, gastronomy and urban planning. The land of the Basques is a vital, optimistic place with an intoxicating spirit.

Without getting drawn into the independence debate, Euskadi (the Basque name for this region) doesn't feel very Spanish. Even the most imperialistic of the Madrid establishment refer to it as 'El País Vasco', the Basque Country. Things are certainly different here; there's a strange language on road signs that would break Scrabble scoring records, weird sports are played to packed houses, it rains an awful lot and a subtle vibrancy infects even the most mundane of daily tasks.

The region's biggest city, Bilbao, has managed superbly to reinvent itself from declining industrial dinosaur to cultured European metropolis. The Guggenheim museum is a powerful symbol of this, but it's the vision that put it there that is even more invigorating. San Sebastián, meanwhile, is perennially popular for its superb natural setting and wonderful gourmet scene, and Vitoria, the peaceful Basque capital, is also very appealing.

Euskadi isn't very large, which means that most rural areas are within easy reach of the three cities. The rugged coast has a few excellent beaches and some very personable fishing ports. Inland, medieval towns still preserve an excellent architectural heritage, while Laguardia, by happy coincidence, is both one of the most attractive walled towns in Northern Spain and an important centre of the Rioja wine region. Outside the towns, the green hills and rocky peaks of this corner of the peninsula are an invitation into the open air.

Andy Symington

Best of
Bilbao &
Basque
Region

top things to do and see

❶ Bilbao's Casco Viejo

Bilbao's compact historic centre slots into a bend in the Nervión River and is an enchanting series of narrow streets surrounding the city's Gothic cathedral. With characterful shops and a great food market, it's a lively zone of commerce and tapas-hopping and the perfect introduction to Bilbao. Page 34.

❷ Museo Guggenheim

Frank Gehry's titanium masterpiece is an unforgettable sight and a powerful symbol of the regeneration of this industrial city and its formerly moribund riverbank area. It's a building to interact with, walking around it and appreciating its perspectives from different angles. Inside, impressive permanent installations are complemented by temporary exhibitions. Page 38.

❸ San Sebastián

A scalloped bay set between craggy headlands, with golden sands and an island feature, give San Sebastián the most postcard-perfect setting of all Spanish cities. Beyond the beaches is an intriguing history and a standout food culture: this is the place that reinvented tapas and made modern peninsular cuisine great. Page 60.

❹ Getaria and Lekeitio

Winding your way along the Basque coastline between Bilbao and San Sebastián is a thrill of character-packed fishing towns, top seafood, spritzy dry whites and some impressive beaches. Getaria and Lekeitio make particularly enticing stops, with picturesque, lively fishing harbours and great coastal scenery. Pages 83 and 88.

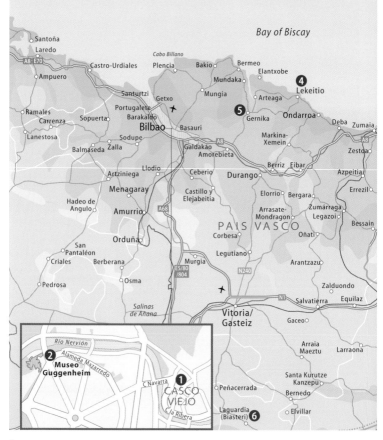

❺ Gernika

The town whose bombing by Nationalist forces in the Civil War inspired Picasso's canvas of the same name and ushered in the era of civilian casualties is no sombre shrine. The spiritual heart of Basque nationalism, it's a vibrant place with an excellent peace museum and lots to see in the surrounding area. Page 90.

❻ Laguardia

One of Spain's most attractive small towns, hilltop Laguardia basks in the sun surrounded by grapevines that produce some of the best Rioja. It makes a superb base for wine tasting and exploring the region. The winning medieval centre features old wine-making cellars dug out under nearly every home. Page 109.

Hondarribia
San Sebastián/
Donostia Pasaie/ Irún
Pasajes
Getaria Renteria
Zarautz
Usurbil Lasarte Hernani Vera
N1
Andoain
Villabona
Tolosa Goizueta Sumbilla
Lizartza Santesteban
Berroeta
A15
Betelu
Lecunberri
Auza
Echarri-
Altsasu- Aranaz Irurzún
Alsasua
Huarte-
Olazagutia Araquil
Zudair

N

10 km
10 miles

When to go

The Basque Country, especially San Sebastián and the coast, is very crowded in July and, especially, August. Prices in beach towns are much higher than normal, though not particularly so in Bilbao. That said, it's an enjoyable time to be in the country as there are dozens of fiestas, and everything happens outdoors. It'll be pleasantly warm rather than baking hot, unless you venture down to the Rioja Alavesa in the south of the region.

June is a good time too, with milder weather and far fewer crowds, as Spanish holidays haven't started. Spring (apart from Easter week) is also quiet, and not too hot, although expect coastal showers if not serious rain. Autumn is a good all-round time. Prices on the coast are slashed (although many hotels shut), and there are few tourists. The weather is unpredictable at this time: you could get a week of warm sun or a fortnight of unrelenting drizzle. A bonus is that flights are cheap at these times.

In winter, temperatures are mild on the coast but often wet. Accommodation is cheaper at this time.

Festivals

Even the smallest village has a fiesta, and some have several. Although mostly nominally religious in nature, they usually include the works; a mass and procession or two to be sure, but also live music, bullfights, competitions, fireworks and copious drinking of *calimocho/kalimotxo*, a mix of red wine and cola (not as bad as it sounds). A feature of many are the *gigantes y cabezudos*, huge-headed papier-mâché figures based on historical personages who parade the streets. Adding to the sense of fun are *peñas*, boisterous social clubs who patrol the streets making music, get rowdy at the bullfights and drink wine all night and day. Most fiestas are in summer, and if you're spending much time in Spain in that period you're bound to run into one; expect some trouble finding accommodation. Details of the major fiestas can be found under Festivals in Listings of individual towns and cities. National holidays and long weekends (*puentes*) can be difficult times to travel; it's important to reserve tickets in advance.

What to do

Birdwatching

The Basque Region is a good place for birding, and where you go is largely determined by what birds you wish to observe. Spain is an important staging post on the migration routes between Africa and Northern Europe/the Arctic. Alava has some worthwhile spots, mostly lakes where vast flocks stop in for refreshment. See www.spainbirds.com for information on birding and nature tours.

Bullfighting

The bullfight, or *corrida*, is an emblem of Spanish culture, a reminder of Roman times when gladiators fought wild beasts in amphitheatres. It is emphatically not a sport (the result is a given) but a ritual; a display of courage by both animal and human (there are and have been several female *toreros*, although it remains a male-dominated field). While to outside observers it can seem uncomfortably like the bull is being humiliated, that is not the way many Spaniards perceive it. Many are contemptuous of the foreign anti-bullfighting lobby, whom they see as meddling hypocrites, but there is significant opposition to the activity within the country (it was banned in Catalunya in 2010 and has also been suspended in several other towns and areas of Spain), mainly in large cities.

The fighting bull, or *toro de lidia*, is virtually a wild animal reared in vast ranches where human contact is minimal.

In a standard bullfight there are six bulls and three matadors, who fight two each. The fights take 15 minutes each, so a standard *corrida* lasts about two hours, usually starting in the late afternoon. The fight is divided into three parts, or *tercios*. In the first part, the bull emerges, and is then played with the cape by the matador, who judges its abilities and tendencies. The bull is then induced to charge a mounted *picador*, who meets it with a sharp lance, which is dug into the bull's neck muscles as it tries to toss the horse.

The second *tercio* involves the placing of three pairs of darts, or *banderillas*, in the bull's neck muscles, to tire it so that the head is low enough to allow the matador to reach the point where the sword should go in.

The last part is the *tercio de la muerte*, or the third of death. The matador faces the bull with a small cape, called a *muleta*, and a sword. After passing it a few times he'll get it in position for the kill. After profiling (turning side on and pointing the sword at the bull), he aims for a point that should kill the bull almost instantly.

If the crowd have been impressed by the bullfighter's performance, they stand and wave their handkerchiefs at the president of the ring, who may then award one or two ears and, exceptionally, the tail.

Cycling

Many organizations run cycling trips around Northern Spain. The region offers very good cycling, and it's a popular weekend activity in Euskadi. In towns, cyclists are not particularly well catered for, but the situation is slowly improving, with cycle lanes popping up in several cities; free bike stands for citizens to borrow a pair of wheels are also widely available.

Road cycling is a popular spectator sport, with the Vuelta a España in September being one of the sport's three prime European events. It's particularly followed in the Basque Country, where the hilly terrain lends itself to strong thighs. The Euskaltel team has promoted the País Vasco on the world cycling stage. Three different Spanish riders have won it in this millennium.

For more information, see the website of the **Real Federación de Ciclismo en España**, www.rfec.com.

Fishing

The Basque Region has some superb trout and salmon fishing, as immortalized by Hemingway in *Fiesta: The Sun Also Rises*. It's all regulated and you'll need a permit (*permiso de pesca*), usually obtainable from the local Ayuntamiento and valid for two weeks. The **Federación Española de Pesca**, Navas de Tolosa 3, Madrid, T915 328 353, www.fepyc.es, is a good starting point.

Football

The sports daily, *Marca*, is a thick publication dedicated mostly to football, and it's the most widely read paper in Spain. Not far behind comes *As*, also devoted to the game. The conclusion to be drawn is that Spaniards are big on sport, and football is king.

While the main football narrative in Spain revolves around Madrid and Barcelona these days, the Basque clubs have certainly held their own. Athletic Bilbao and Real Sociedad have both won the championship, while Alavés (from Vitoria) and little Eibar have both seen top division action recently.

Going to a game is an excellent experience; crowds are enthusiastic but well behaved, and it's much more of a family affair than in the UK, for example. Games traditionally take place on a Sunday evening (most at 1700) although there are now fixtures spread right through the weekend from Friday to Monday evenings. Tickets are relatively easy to come by for most games. The *taquillas* (ticket booths) are normally open at the ground for two days before the match and for the couple of hours before kick-off. Some, but by no means all, clubs now have ticket sales on their websites.

Watching the big game in a bar is a ritual for many people, and also good fun. The website **www.soccer-spain.com** has good information on the Spanish scene in English.

Golf

The Basque Region doesn't have the concentration of golf courses that you find in Andalucía and the southeast coast, but there are enough quality spots to keep any golfer interested, and the higher rainfall on the north coast makes for a guilt-free swing. You'll need a green card (insurance) and sometimes a handicap certificate to play most of the Basque Region's courses. See **www.golfspain.com** for good course information in English.

Surfing and other watersports

There are good surf beaches right along the coast and the sport is growing in popularity in Spain. There's a big scene around Zarautz and Mundaka (whose left break is world-renowned) in Euskadi. Many of the best surf beaches are listed in the text of this guide.

The north coast is the obvious choice for watersports, with many companies arranging activities in Euskadi. There's some reasonable diving on the Guipúzcoan Coast.

Walking and climbing

The Basque Region offers some fantastic walking, mostly in its mountainous and coastal areas. Spain has an excellent network of marked walking trails, which are divided into **Pequeño Recorrido** (PR) – short trails marked with yellow and white signs – and **Gran Recorrido** (GR) – longer-distance walks marked in red and white. These take in places often inaccessible by car; the GR trails are planned so that nights can be spent at *refugios* (walkers' hostels) or in villages with places to stay. Detailed maps and descriptions of these routes can be found in good bookshops or outdoor equipment shops; web coverage is good for some routes but still patchy overall.

Tourist offices have details of local routes and *refugios*. The most useful website if you can read some Spanish is **www.wikiloc.com**, which can be combined with Google Earth to give a 3D-view of the walking route. The website **www.wikirutas.es** is another great hiking resource; both are available as a smartphone app.

Shopping tips

Although chain stores are rapidly swallowing them up, one of the most endearing aspects of the country is the profusion of small shops, many little changed in recent decades and always family-run. While there are many supermarkets, people buy their bread from bakers, their newspapers from kiosks, their tobacco from tobacconists, and they get their shoes repaired at cobblers. Food markets are still the focus of many towns.

Standard shop opening hours are Monday to Friday 1000-1400 and 1700-2000, and Saturday mornings. Big supermarkets stay open through the lunch hour and shut at 2100 or 2200.

Bargaining is not usual except at markets but it's worth asking for a *descuento* if you're buying in bulk or paying in cash. Non-EU residents can reclaim VAT (*IVA*) on purchases over €90; the easiest way to do this is to get a tax-free cheque from participating shops (look for the sticker), which can then be cashed at customs.

What to buy

Clothing is an obvious choice; Spanish fashion is strong. While the larger chains have branched out into Britain and beyond, there are many smaller stores with good ranges of gear that you won't be able to get outside the country. Bilbao is the best place, but every medium-sized town will have plenty on offer.

Leather is another good buy; jackets tend to be at least 30% less than in the UK, although the range of styles available isn't as great. There are plenty of places that will make bespoke leather goods. **Shoes** are fairly well priced and unusual.

Ceramics are a good choice: cheap, attractive and practical in the most part.

Local **fiestas** usually have handicraft markets attached to them; these can be excellent places to shop, as artisans from all around the region bring their wares to town; you'll soon distinguish the real ones from the imported mass-produced versions.

An obvious choice is **food**. Ham keeps well and is cheap. Chorizo is a tasty, portable alternative. Most shops will vacuum-pack these things for you: ask for *envasado al vacío*. *Aceitunas con anchoa* (olives stuffed with anchovies) are a cheap and packable choice, as is the range of quality canned and marinated seafood.

Spanish wine is another good purchase. However, the price differential with the UK is only about 30% so try to find bottles that you can't get at home. **Spirits** are significantly cheaper than in most of Europe; a bottle of gin from London, for example, can in Spain cost as little as 50% of the British price. A good souvenir is a *bota*, the goatskin wine bags used at fiestas and bullfights. Try and buy one from a *botería*, the traditional workshops where they are made, rather than at a tourist shop.

Cigars (*puros*) can be as little as a tenth of UK prices, and there's a large range in many tobacconists (*estancos*). **Cigarettes**, meanwhile, are cheaper too; about €4.75 a packet for most international brands. They're cheaper on the street than at airports.

ON THE ROAD

Improve your travel photography

Taking pictures is a highlight for many travellers, yet too often the results turn out to be disappointing. Steve Davey, author of Footprint's *Travel Photography*, sets out his top rules for coming home with pictures you can be proud of.

Before you go

Don't waste precious travelling time and do your research before you leave. Find out what festivals or events might be happening or which day the weekly market takes place, and search online image sites such as Flickr to see whether places are best shot at the beginning or end of the day, and what vantage points you should consider.

Get up early

The quality of the light will be better in the few hours after sunrise and again before sunset – especially in the tropics when the sun will be harsh and unforgiving in the middle of the day. Sometimes seeing the sunrise is a part of the whole travel experience: sleep in and you will miss more than just photographs.

Stop and think

Don't just click away without any thought. Pause for a few seconds before raising the camera and ask yourself what you are trying to show with your photograph. Think about what things you need to include in the frame to convey this meaning. Be prepared to move around your subject to get the best angle. Knowing the point of your picture is the first step to making sure that the person looking at the picture will know it too.

Compose your picture

Avoid simply dumping your subject in the centre of the frame every time you take a picture. If you compose with it to one side, then your picture can look more balanced. This will also allow you to show a significant background and make the picture more meaningful. A good rule of thumb is to place your subject or any significant detail a third of the way into the frame; facing into the frame not out of it.

This rule also works for landscapes. Compose with the horizon two-thirds of the way up the frame if the foreground is the most interesting part of the picture; one-third of the way up if the sky is more striking.

Don't get hung up with this so-called Rule of Thirds, though. Exaggerate it by pushing your subject out to the edge of the frame if it makes a more interesting picture; or if the sky is dull in a landscape, try cropping with the horizon near the very top of the frame.

Fill the frame

If you are going to focus on a detail or even a person's face in a close-up portrait, then be bold and make sure that you fill the frame. This is often a case of physically getting in close. You can use a telephoto setting on a zoom lens but this can lead to pictures looking quite flat; moving in close is a lot more fun!

Interact with people

If you want to shoot evocative portraits then it is vital to approach people and seek permission in some way, even if it is just by smiling at someone. Spend a little time with them and they are likely to relax and look less stiff and formal. Action portraits where people are doing something, or environmental portraits, where they are set against a significant background, are a good way to achieve relaxed portraits. Interacting is a good way to find out more about people and their lives, creating memories as well as photographs.

Focus carefully

Your camera can focus quicker than you, but it doesn't know which part of the picture you want to be in focus. If your camera is using the centre focus sensor then move the camera so it is over the subject and half press the button, then, holding it down, recompose the picture. This will lock the focus. Take the now correctly focused picture when you are ready.

Another technique for accurate focusing is to move the active sensor over your subject. Some cameras with touch-sensitive screens allow you to do this by simply clicking on the subject.

Leave light in the sky

Most good night photography is actually taken at dusk when there is some light and colour left in the sky; any lit portions of the picture will balance with the sky and any ambient lighting. There is only a very small window when this will happen, so get into position early, be prepared and keep shooting and reviewing the results. You can take pictures after this time, but avoid shots of tall towers in an inky black sky; crop in close on lit areas to fill the frame.

Bring it home safely

Digital images are inherently ephemeral: they can be deleted or corrupted in a heartbeat. The good news though is they can be copied just as easily. Wherever you travel, you should have a backup strategy. Cloud backups are popular, but make sure that you will have access to fast enough Wi-Fi. If you use RAW format, then you will need some sort of physical back-up. If you don't travel with a laptop or tablet, then you can buy a backup drive that will copy directly from memory cards.

Recently updated and available in both digital and print formats, Footprint's Travel Photography by Steve Davey covers everything you need to know about travelling with a camera, including simple post-processing. More information is available at www.footprinttravelguides.com

Where to stay

remote refugios and countryside casas rurales

There are a reasonable number of well-equipped but characterless places on the edges or in the newer parts of towns. Similarly, chains such as NH, AC, Meliá and Hesperia have stocked Spain's cities with reasonably comfortable but frequently featureless four-star business hotels. This guide has expressly minimized these in the listings, preferring to concentrate on more atmospheric options, but they are easily accessible via their websites or hotel booking brokers. These things change, but at time of writing, by far the best booking website for accommodation in Spain was www.booking.com. The standard of accommodation in the Basque Country is very high; even the most modest of *pensiones* are usually very clean and respectable. Places to stay (*alojamientos*) are divided into three main categories; the distinctions between them follow an arcane series of regulations devised by the government.

All registered accommodations charge a 10% value-added tax (IVA); this is usually included in the price and may be waived if you pay cash. If you have any problems, a last resort is to ask for the *libro de reclamaciones* (complaints book), an official document that means uncertain but definitely horrible consequences for the hotel if anything is written in it. If you do write something in it, you have to go to the police within 24 hours and report the fact.

Price codes

Where to stay		Restaurants	
€€€€	over €170	€€€	over €25
€€€	€110-170	€€	€15-25
€€	€60-110	€	under €15
€	under €60		

These price codes refer to a standard double/twin room, inclusive of the 10% IVA (value-added tax). The rates are for high season (usually Jun-Aug).

Price refers to the cost of a main course for one person, without a drink.

Hoteles, hostales and pensiones

Hoteles (marked H or HR) are graded from one to five stars and usually occupy their own building. *Hostales* (marked Hs or HsR) are cheaper guesthouse-style places that go from one to three stars. *Pensiones* (P) are the standard budget option, and are usually family-run flats in an apartment block. Although it's worth looking at a room before taking it, the majority are very acceptable. Spanish traditions of hospitality are alive and well; even the simplest of *pensiones* will generally provide a towel and soap, and check-out time is almost uniformly a very civilized midday. Most *pensiones* will give you keys to the exterior door; if they don't, be sure to mention the fact if you plan to stay out late to check that there'll be someone to open it for you.

Agroturismos and casas rurales

An excellent option if you've got transport are the networks of rural homes, called a variety of names, normally *agroturismos* or *casas rurales*. Although these are under a different classification system, the standard is often as high as any country hotel. The best of them are traditional farmhouses or old village cottages. Some are available only to rent out whole, while others operate more or less as hotels. Rates tend to be excellent compared to hotels, and many offer kitchen facilities and home-cooked meals. This can be a hugely relaxing form of holiday accommodation and a great way to meet Spaniards.

While many are listed in the text, there are huge numbers, especially in the coastal and mountain areas. The Basque tourist board publishes a list of them, available in tourist offices or searchable on their website www.turismo.euskadi.net. The website www.nekatur.net is also a useful resource.

Albergues and refugios

There are a few youth hostels (*albergues*) around, but the accessible price of *pensiones* rarely makes it worth the trouble except for solo travellers. Spanish youth hostels are frequently populated by noisy schoolkids and have curfews and check-out times unsuitable for the late hours the locals keep.

Campsites

Most campsites are set up as well-equipped holiday villages for families; many are open only in summer. While the facilities are good, they get extremely busy in peak season; the social scene is lively, but sleep can be tough. They've often got playground facilities and a swimming pool; an increasing number offer cabin or bungalow accommodation, normally a good-value option for groups or families. In other areas, camping, unless specifically prohibited, is a matter of common sense.

Food
& drink

Basque pintxos and txakolí wine

Nothing in Spain illustrates its differences from the rest of Europe more than its eating and drinking culture. Whether you're winding down Sunday lunch at 1800, ordering a plate of octopus some time after midnight, snacking on *pintxos* in the street with the entire population of Bilbao doing the same around you, or watching a businessman down a hefty brandy with his morning coffee, it hits you at some point that the whole of Spanish society more or less revolves around food and drink. Nowhere is this more so than in the Basque Country, Spain's gastronomic paradise and a place that has taken bar snacking to gourmet extremes.

Eating hours are the first point of difference. Spaniards eat little for breakfast, usually just a coffee and maybe a croissant or pastry. The mid-morning coffee and piece of tortilla is a ritual, especially for office workers, and then there might be a quick bite and a drink in a bar before lunch, which is usually started between 1400 and 1530. This is the main meal of the day and the cheapest time to eat, as most restaurants offer a good-value set menu. Lunch (and dinner) is extended at weekends, particularly on Sundays, when the *sobremesa* (chatting over the remains of the meal) can go on for hours. Most folk head home for the meal during the working week and get back to work about 1700; some people have a nap (the famous siesta), some don't. It's common to have an evening drink or *pintxo* in a bar after a stroll, or *paseo*: if this is extended into a food crawl it's called a *txikiteo*. Dinner (*cena*) is normally eaten from about 2130 onwards. Be aware that any restaurant open for dinner before 2030 could well be a tourist trap. After eating, *la marcha* (the nightlife) hits drinking bars (*bares de copas*) and then nightclubs (*discotecas*; a *club* is a brothel). Many of these places only open at weekends and are usually busiest from 0100 onwards.

Week nights are quieter in the Basque Country, where many restaurants close their kitchens at 2200.

While the regional differences in Basque cuisine are important, the basics remain the same right across the peninsula. Spanish cooking relies on meat, fish/seafood, beans and potatoes given character by the chef's holy trinity: garlic, peppers and, of course, olive oil. The influence of the colonization of the Americas is evident, and the result is a hearty, filling style of meal ideally washed down with some of the nation's excellent red wines.

The availability of good **fish and seafood** can be taken for granted. *Merluza* (hake) is the staple fish, but is pushed hard by *bacalao* (salt cod). *Besugo* (sea-bream), *lenguado* (sole), *dorada* (gilthead bream) and *lubina* (sea bass) are ubiquitous, and a variety of farmed white fish are also increasingly popular. *Gambas* (prawns) are another common and excellent choice, backed up by a bewildering array of molluscs and crustaceans as well as numerous tasty fish. Calamari, squid and cuttlefish are common; if you can cope with the slightly slimy texture, *pulpo* (octopus) is particularly good, especially when simply boiled *a la gallega* (Galician style) and flavoured with paprika and olive oil. Supreme among the seafood are *rodaballo* (turbot) and *rape* (monkfish/anglerfish).

Wherever you go, you'll find cured ham (*jamón serrano*), which is always excellent, but particularly so if it's the pricey *ibérico*, taken from acorn-eating porkers in Salamanca, Extremadura and Huelva. Other cold **meats** to look out for are *cecina*, made from beef and, of course, *embutidos* (sausages), including the versatile *chorizo* and the typically Basque *txistorra*. Pork is also popular as a cooked meat; its most common form is sliced loin (*lomo*). Beef is common throughout; cheaper cuts predominate, but the better steaks (*solomillo, entrecot, chuletón*) are usually superbly tender. Spaniards tend to eat them rare (*poco hecho*; ask for *al punto* for medium-rare or *bien hecho* for well done). The *chuletón* is worth a mention in its own right; a massive T-bone best taken from an ox (*de buey*) and sold by weight, which often approaches a kilogram. It's an imposing slab of meat, best shared between two or three unless you're especially peckish. *Pollo* (chicken) is common, but usually unremarkable (unless it's free-range – *pollo de corral* – in which case it's superb); game birds such as *codorniz* (quail) and *perdiz* (partridge) as well as *pato* (duck) are also widely eaten. The innards of animals are popular; *callos* (tripe), *mollejas* (sweetbreads), *oreja* (ear) and *morcilla* (black pudding) are all excellent, if acquired, tastes.

Main dishes often come without any **accompaniments**, or chips at best. The consolation, however, is the *ensalada mixta*, whose simple name (mixed salad) often conceals a meal in itself. The ingredients vary, but it's typically a plentiful combination of lettuce, tomato, onion, olive oil, boiled eggs, asparagus, olives and tuna. The tortilla (a substantial potato omelette) is ever-present and often excellent. *Revueltos* (scrambled egg or stir-fried dishes), are usually tastily combined with prawns, asparagus or other goodies. Most **vegetable** dishes are based around that New World trio: the bean, the pepper and the potato. There are numerous varieties of bean in Northern Spain; they are normally served as some sort of hearty stew, often with bits of meat or seafood. Peppers (*pimientos*), too, come in a number of forms. As well as being used to flavour dishes, they are often eaten in their own right; *pimientos rellenos* come stuffed with meat or seafood. Potatoes come as chips, *bravas* (with a garlic or spicy tomato sauce) or *a la riojana*, with chorizo and paprika. Other common vegetable dishes include *menestra* (delicious blend of cooked vegetables), which usually has some ham in it, and *ensaladilla rusa*, a tasty blend of potato, peas, peppers, carrots and mayonnaise. *Setas* (wild mushrooms) are a delight, particularly in autumn.

Desserts focus on the sweet and milky. *Flan* (a sort of crème caramel) is ubiquitous; great when *casero* (home-made), but often out of a plastic tub. *Natillas* are a similar but more liquid version, and *arroz con leche* is a cold, sweet, rice pudding typical of Northern Spain. **Cheeses** are normally eaten as a tapa or entrée. Though the standard Manchego-style cheese is still the staple of its kind (it comes *semi-curado*, semi-cured, or *curado* – much stronger and tastier), there are a number of interesting regional cheeses that are well worth trying. Idiázabal stands out among Basque varieties.

Basque cuisine

Regional styles tend to use the same basic ingredients treated in slightly different ways, backed up by some local specialities. Most of Spain grudgingly concedes that Basque cuisine is the peninsula's best, the San Sebastián twilight shimmers with Michelin stars, and chummy all-male *txokos* gather in private to swap recipes and cook up feasts in members-only kitchens. But what strikes the visitor first are the *pintxos*, a stunning range of bartop snacks that in many cases seem too pretty to put your teeth in. But what you see arrayed along the bartop is only half the story. Many bars have a huge range of cooked-to-order hot *pintxos*, which showcase the best that kitchen has to offer (see box, page 50). The base of most Basque dishes is seafood, particularly *bacalao* (salt cod), and the region has taken full advantage of its French ties. Classic Basque cod dishes include *bacalao a la vizcaína*, where the fish is steamed in a tomato, red pepper and onion sauce, and *bacalao al pil-pil*, where a thick yellow sauce is produced by gelatin from the fish skin combining with oil and garlic.

Other Basque specialities include stuffed *txangurro* (spider crab), *marmitako*, a hearty stew of *bonito* (tuna) and potatoes, and *porrusalda*, a stew of leeks and other vegetables. The famous black beans from Tolosa are another base for deliciously heavy winter dishes.

Food-producing regions take their responsibilities seriously, and competition is fierce. Those widely acknowledged to produce the best will often add the name of the region to the foodstuff (many foods, like wines, have denomination of origin status, DO, given by a regulatory body).

Eating out

One of the great pleasures of travelling in the Basque Country is eating out, but it's no fun sitting in an empty restaurant so adapt to the local hours as much as you can; it may feel strange leaving dinner until 2130, but you'll miss out on a lot of atmosphere if you don't.

The standard distinctions of bar, café and restaurant don't apply in Spain. Many places combine all three functions, and it's not always evident; the dining room (*comedor*) is often tucked away behind the bar or upstairs. *Restaurantes* are restaurants, and will usually have a dedicated dining area with set menus and à la carte options. Bars and cafés will display food on the counter, or have a list of *pintxos*; bars tend to be known for particular dishes they do well. Many bars, cafés and restaurants don't open on Sunday nights, and most are closed one other night a week, most commonly Monday or Tuesday.

Cafés will usually provide some kind of **breakfast** fare in the mornings; croissants and sweet pastries are the norm; freshly squeezed orange juice is also common. About 1100 they start putting out savoury fare; maybe a tortilla, some *ensaladilla rusa* or little ham rolls in preparation for pre-lunch snacking. It's a workers' tradition – from labourers to executives – to drop down to the local bar around 1130 for a *pincho de tortilla* (slice of potato omelette) to get them through until lunchtime.

Lunch is the biggest meal of the day for most people in Spain, and it's also the cheapest time to eat. Just about all restaurants offer a *menú del día*, which is usually a set three-course meal that includes wine or soft drink. In unglamorous workers' locals this is often as little as €10; paying anything more than €15 indicates the restaurant takes itself quite seriously. There's often a choice of several starters and mains. To make the most of the meal, a tip is to order another starter in place of a main; most places are quite happy to do it, and the starters are usually more interesting than the mains, which in the cheaper places tend to be slabs of mediocre meat. Most places open for lunch at about 1300, and stop serving at 1500 or 1530, although at weekends this can extend; it's not uncommon to see people still lunching at 1800 on a Sunday. The quality of à la carte is usually higher than the *menú*, and quantities are larger. Simpler restaurants won't offer this option except

Menu reader

aceite oil; *aceite de oliva* is olive oil
aceitunas olives, also called *olivas*
ahumado smoked
ajo garlic, *ajetes* are young garlic shoots
ajo arriero a simple sauce of garlic, paprika and parsley
albóndigas meatballs
alcachofa artichoke
alcaparras capers
alioli a sauce of raw garlic blended with oil and egg yolk; also called *ajoaceite*
almejas clams
alubias con chorizo a typical regional dish of chorizo and beans
anchoa preserved anchovy
arroz rice; *arroz con leche* is a sweet rice pudding
asado roast
atún blue-fin tuna
bacalao salt cod, *al pil-pil* is salt cod in a light yellow sauce made from oil and garlic
berberechos cockles
bistek cheap steak
bocadillo/bocata a crusty filled roll
bogavante lobster
boletus porcini mushrooms
bonito Atlantic bonito, a small tuna fish
boquerones fresh anchovies
brasa (a la) cooked on a griddle over coals
buey ox
cabrito young goat, usually roasted (*asado*)
calamares squid
caldereta a stew of meat or fish
caldo a thickish soup
callos tripe
cangrejo crab; occasionally river crayfish
carne meat
cazuela a stew, often of fish or seafood
cecina cured beef like a leathery ham
cerdo pork

chipirones small squid
chuleta/chuletilla chop
chuletón massive T-bone steak
churrasco barbecued meat
churro a fried dough-stick usually eaten with hot chocolate (*chocolate con churros*)
cigalas Dublin Bay prawn/langoustines
cochinillo/lechón/tostón suckling pig
cocido a heavy stew, usually of chickpeas or beans with meat and vegetables; *sopa de cocido* is the broth
conejo rabbit
cordero lamb
crema catalana a lemony *crème brûlée*
croquetas deep-fried crumbed balls of meat, béchamel, seafood, or vegetables
dorada a species of bream (gilthead)
embutido any salami-type sausage
empanada a savoury pie, sold by the slice
ensalada salad; *mixta* is lettuce, tomato, onion, olive oil, boiled eggs, asparagus, olives and tuna
ensaladilla rusa Russian salad, with potato, peas and carrots in mayonnaise
entrecot sirloin steak
erizos/ericios sea urchins
escabeche pickled in wine and vinegar
espárragos asparagus, usually canned
estofado braised, often in stew form
fideuá a bit like a paella but with noodles
filete a cheap cut of steak
flan crème caramel
frito/a fried
gambas prawns
garbanzos chickpeas
guisado stewed, or a stew
guisantes peas
habas broad beans
helado ice cream
hígado liver

in the evenings. **Tapas** has changed in meaning over the years, and now basically refers to all bar food. This range includes *pinchos/pintxos* (see box, page 50), and more substantial dishes, usually ordered in *raciones* and designed to be shared. A *ración* in Northern Spain is no mean affair; it can often comfortably fill one

horno (al) oven (baked)
huevo egg
ibérico See *jamón*
jabalí wild boar, usually found in autumn
jamón ham; *jamón York* is cooked British-style ham, but much better is the cured *serrano*; *ibérico* refers to ham from the Iberian breed of pigs that are fed partly on acorns (*bellotas*)
kokotxas pieces of hake cheek and throat, cooked in a rich sauce; usually delicious
langosta crayfish
langostinos king prawns
lechazo milk-fed lamb
lenguado sole
lentejas lentils
lomo loin, usually sliced pork
lubina sea bass
mantequilla butter
manzanilla a type of olive; also camomile tea; and a dry wine similar to sherry
marisco shellfish
mejillones mussels
membrillo quince jelly
menestra a vegetable stew, served like minestrone without the liquid
merluza hake
mero grouper
migas breadcrumbs, fried in lard
mollejas sweetbreads
morcilla blood sausage
nata sweet whipped cream
navajas razor-shells
orejas ears, usually of a pig
ostra oyster
pan bread
parrilla grill; a *parrillada* is a mixed grill
pastel cake/pastry
patatas potatoes; often chips (*patatas fritas*); *bravas* are with spicy sauce; *a la riojana* is with paprika and chorizo

pato duck
percebes goose-neck barnacles
pescado fish
picadillo a dish of spicy minced pork
picante spicy
pimientos peppers; *piquillos* are thin Basque red pepper; Padrón produces sweet green mini ones
pintxo/pincho a bar-top snack
plancha (a la) grilled on a hot iron
pochas young haricot beans
pollo chicken
postre dessert
pulga tiny submarine-shaped rolls
pulpo octopus, *a la gallega*, boiled Galician style
queso cheese
rabas crumbed calamari strips
rabo de buey oxtail
rape monkfish/anglerfish
relleno/a stuffed
revuelto scrambled eggs
rodaballo turbot; pricey and delicious
romana (a la) fried in batter
salchichón a salami-like sausage
salpicón a seafood salad
San Jacobo steak with ham and cheese
sepia cuttlefish
setas wild mushrooms
solomillo beef fillet steak
tarta tart or cake
ternera young beef
tocino pork fat; *tocinillo del cielo* is an excellent caramelized egg dessert
toro a traditional Basque fish stew or soup
trucha trout
txaka/chaka a mix of mayonnaise and seafood, featuring in *pintxos*
verduras vegetables
vieiras scallops, also called *veneras*
zamburiñas queen scallop

person, so if you want to sample a range of things, you're better to ask for a half (*media*). Prices of *raciones* basically depend on the ingredients; a good portion of *langostinos* (king prawns) will likely set you back €15, while more *morcilla* (black pudding) or *patatas* than you can eat might only be €5 or so.

Most restaurants open for dinner at 2030 or later. In these straitened economic times in Spain, restaurants are increasingly offering a *menú de noche*, a set evening meal that can be a real boon for the traveller. Midweek in the Basque Country, restaurants are often closing by 2200, but at weekends many people sit down to dinner substantially later than that. A cheap option at all times is a *plato combinado*, most commonly offered in cafés. They're usually a greasy spoon-style mix of eggs, steak, bacon and chips or similar and are filling but rarely inspiring.

Vegetarians won't be spoiled for choice, but at least what there is tends to be good, and the Basque Country is more vegetarian-friendly than other parts of Spain. There's a small but rapidly increasing number of dedicated vegetarian restaurants, but most other places won't have a vegetarian main course on offer, although the existence of *raciones* and salads makes this less of a burden than it might be. *Ensalada mixta* nearly always has tuna in it, but it's usually made fresh, so places will happily leave it out. *Ensaladilla rusa* is normally a good bet, but ask about the tuna too, just in case. Tortilla is simple but delicious and ubiquitous. Simple potato or pepper dishes are tasty options (although beware of peppers stuffed with meat), and many *revueltos* (scrambled eggs and stirfries) are meat-free. Annoyingly, most vegetable *menestras* are seeded with ham before cooking, and bean dishes usually contain at least some meat or animal fat. You'll have to specify *soy vegetariano/a* (I am a vegetarian), but ask what dishes contain, as ham, fish and chicken are often considered suitable vegetarian fare. **Vegans** will have a tougher time. What doesn't have meat nearly always contains cheese or egg, though a *parrillada de verduras* (mixed grilled vegetables) is an increasingly common option in restaurants. Better restaurants, particularly in cities, will be happy to prepare something to guidelines, but otherwise better stick to very simple dishes. *Setas* (wild mushrooms) are widely available.

Drink

In good Catholic fashion, **wine** is the lifeblood of Spain. It's the standard accompaniment to most meals, but also features very prominently in bars, where a glass of cheap *tinto* or *blanco* can cost as little as €0.80, although it's more normally €1.50-2. A bottle of cheap house wine in a simple restaurant is often no more than €5 or €6. *Tinto* is red (although if you just order *vino* it's assumed that's what you want; a *txikito* is a glass of basic red wine, much ordered on the *pintxo* trail); *blanco* is white, and rosé is either *clarete* or *rosado*. A well-regulated system of *denominaciones de origen* (DO), similar to the French *appelation controlée*, has lifted the reputation of Spanish wines high above the party plonk status they once enjoyed. Recent years have seen regions such as the Ribera del Duero, Rueda, Toro, Bierzo, and Rías Baixas achieve worldwide recognition. But the daddy, of course, is still Rioja, a good proportion of which is produced in the Basque Country.

The overall standard of Riojas has improved markedly since the granting of the higher DOC status in 1991, with some fairly stringent testing in place. Red predominates; these are mostly medium-bodied bottles from the Tempranillo grape (with three other permitted red grapes often used to add depth or character). Whites from Viura and Malvasia are also produced: the majority of these are young, fresh and dry, unlike the traditional powerful oaky Rioja whites now on the decline. Rosés are also produced. The quality of individual Riojas varies widely according to both producer and the amount of time the wines have been aged in oak barrels and in the bottle. The words *crianza*, *reserva* and *gran reserva* refer to the length of the ageing process, while the vintage date is also given. Rioja producers store their wines at the bodega until deemed ready for drinking, so it's common to see wines dating back a decade or more on shelves and wine lists.

Many people feel, however, that Spain's best reds come from further west, in the Ribera del Duero region east of Valladolid. The royal family's favourite tipple, Vega Sicilia, has long been Spain's most prestigious wine, but other producers from the area have also gained stellar reviews. The intense summer heat of nearby Toro makes for traditional, full-bodied reds, but some more subtle wines of striking quality have emerged from there recently, including Vega Sicilia-owned Pintia.

Visiting the area in the baking summer heat, it's hard to believe that nearby Rueda can produce quality whites, but it certainly does. Most come from the Verdejo grape and have an attractive, dry, lemony taste; Sauvignon Blanc has also been planted with some success.

Galicia produces some excellent whites too; the coastal Albariño vineyards produce a sought-after dry but fruity wine with a very distinctive bouquet.

ON THE ROAD
Getting to grips with the grapes

Calimocho The drink of choice for students and revellers, red wine mixed 50-50 with Coca-Cola. Often served in *cachis*, paper cups holding a litre that are designed to be shared.

Cava Sparkling wine, mostly produced in Catalunya.

Cosechero A young red from the latest vintage.

Crianza Must be at least two years old, at least six months of which have been spent in oak (12 months in the case of Rioja).

DO *Denominación de origen* is a regional wine appellation controlled by a regulatory body. Rioja is a DOC (*denominación de origen calificada*), with extra strictures. DO status also exists for other products.

Fresco Most bars will keep some bottles of red *fresco*, or chilled; a refreshing option in summer.

Gran reserva The softest and most characterful of Spanish wines, although sometimes tending to be over-aged. At least five years old, with two or more in oak. Only produced in good years.

Mosto Grape juice, a common option in bars.

Reserva A red which has passed its third birthday, of which 12 months (often more) have been in oak.

Tinto de verano A refreshing summer mix of cheap red wine, ice and lemonade.

Txakolí A slightly effervescent Basque wine produced from underripe grapes

Vino Wine; *blanco* is white, *rosado* or *clarete* is rosé, *tinto* is red.

Vino corriente/normal/de mesa The cheap option in bars and restaurants, table wine that can vary from terrible to reasonable. Often high in acid, which balances the oily Spanish food. Served in a tumbler in bars so there's no pretending. Restaurants will often provide *gaseosa*, a form of lemonade, to mix with it.

Vino generoso 'Generous', ie fortified, wine, such as sherry.

Ribeiro is another good Galician white, and the reds from there are also tasty, having some similarity to those produced in nearby northern Portugal. Ribeira Sacra is another inland Galician denomination producing whites and reds from a wide range of varietals.

Among other regions, Navarra, long known only for rosé, produces some quality red wines unfettered by the stricter rules governing production in Rioja, while Bierzo, in western León province, also produces interesting wines from the red Prieto Picudo and Mencía grapes. Other DO wines in Northern Spain include Somontano, a red and white appellation from Aragón and Toro, whose baking climate makes for full-bodied reds. Some Toro wines have achieved a very high worldwide profile.

An unusual wine worth trying is *txakolí*, with a small production on the Basque coast. The most common is a young, refreshing, acidic white which has a green tinge and slight sparkle, often accentuated by pouring from a height. The best examples, from around Getaria, go well with seafood. The wine is made from under-ripe grapes of the Ondarrubi Zuria variety; there's a less common red species and some rosé.

One of the joys of Spain, though, is the rest of the wine. Order a *menú del día* at a cheap restaurant and you'll be unceremoniously served a cheap bottle of local red (sometimes without even asking for it). Wine snobbery can leave by the back door at this point: it may be cold, but you'll find it refreshing; it may be acidic, but once the olive-oil laden food arrives, you'll be glad of it. It's not there to be judged, it's a staple like bread and, like bread, it's sometimes excellent, it's sometimes bad, but mostly it fulfils its purpose perfectly. Wine is not a luxury item in Spain, so people add water to it if they feel like it, or lemonade (*gaseosa*), or *cola* (to make the party drink called *calimocho*). *Tinto de verano* is a summer slurper similar to sangria, a mixture of red wine, *gaseosa*, ice, and optional fruit.

In most bars, you can order Rioja, Ribera, Rueda, or other regions by the glass (usually €1.20-2.50). If you ask for *crianza* or *reserva*, you'll usually get a Rioja. A *tinto* or *blanco* will usually get you a cheapish local wine, sometimes excellent, sometimes awful. As a general rule, only bars serving food serve wine; most *pubs* and *discotecas* won't have it.

Spanish **beer** is mostly lager, usually reasonably strong, fairly gassy, cold and good. On the Basque *pintxo* trail, many people order *zuritos*, usually about 100 ml. A *caña* is a regular draught beer, usually about 200 ml. Order a *cerveza* and you'll get a bottled beer. Many people order their beer *con gas* (half beer and half fizzy sweet water) or *con limón* (half lemonade, also called a *clara*). In some pubs, particularly those specializing in different beers (*cervecerías*), you can order pints (*pintas*). In these, local craft beers are beginning to make an appearance, and lots of them stock a wide range of imported options in bottles.

Cider (*sidra*) is another popular Basque drink. In Euskadi in springtime, people decamp to cider houses in the hills to eat massive meals and serve themselves bottomless glasses of the stuff direct from the vat.

Spirits are cheap in Spain. Vermouth (*vermut*) is a popular pre-lunch *aperitif*, as is *patxarán*. Many bars make their own vermouth by adding various herbs and fruits and letting it sit in barrels; this can be excellent, particularly if it's from a *solera*. This is a system where liquid is drawn from the oldest of a series of barrels, which is then topped up with the next oldest, resulting in a very mellow characterful drink. After dinner or lunch it's time for a *copa*: people relax over a whisky or a brandy, or hit the mixed drinks (*cubatas*): *gin tonic* is obvious, as is *vodka con cola*. Spirits are free-poured and large; don't be surprised at a 100-ml measure. A mixed drink costs €4-7. The range of gins, in particular, is extraordinary. There's always a good selection of rum (*ron*) and blended whisky available too. Spanish brandy is good, although its oaky vanilla flavours don't appeal to everyone. When ordering a spirit, you'll be expected to choose which brand you want; the local varieties (eg **Larios** gin, **DYC** whisky) are sometimes marginally cheaper than their imported brethren but lower in quality.

Juice is normally bottled and expensive; *mosto* (grape juice; really pre-fermented wine) is a cheaper and popular soft drink in bars. There's the usual range of **fizzy drinks** (*gaseosas*) available. *Horchata* is a summer drink, a sort of smoothie made from tiger nuts. **Water** (*agua*) comes *con* (with) or *sin* (without) *gas*. The tap water is totally safe to drink.

Coffee (*café*) is usually excellent and strong. *Solo* is black, mostly served espresso style. Order *americano* if you want a long black, *cortado* if you want a dash of milk, or *con leche* for about half milk. A *carajillo* is a coffee with brandy. **Tea** (*té*) is served without milk unless you ask; herbal teas (*infusiones*) are common, especially chamomile (*manzanilla*) and mint (*menta poleo*). **Chocolate** is a reasonably popular drink at breakfast time or in the afternoon (*merienda*), served with *churros*, fried doughsticks that seduce about a quarter of visitors and repel the rest.

Bilbao/
Bilbo

Bilbao/Bilbo

Dirty industrial city turned buzzing cultural capital: Bilbao is a byword for urban renewal. The Guggenheim museum is the undoubted flagship of this triumphant progress, a sinuous fantasy of a building that will take your breath away. While the museum has led the turnaround, much of what is enjoyable about modern Bilbao was already there: bustling bar life, harmonious old and new architecture, a superb eating culture, and a tangible sense of pride in being a working city.

The Casco Viejo still evokes a cramped medieval past. Along its web of attractive streets, designer clothing stores occupy the ground floors where families perhaps once huddled behind the city walls. El Ensanche, the new town, has an elegant European feel to it with stately banks and classy shops lining the planned avenues. The riverbank is the most obvious beneficiary of Bilbao's renaissance: Calatrava's eerily skeletal bridge, designer promenades and Gehry's exuberant Guggenheim bring art and architecture together and make the Nervión river and estuary the city's axis once more.

The seaside suburbs are 20 minutes away by metro. Fashionable Getxo has a relaxed beach atmosphere, while across the estuary, Portugalete still seems to be wondering how Bilbao gets all the credit these days: for hundreds of years it was a far more important port.

Essential Bilbao/Bilbo

Finding your feet

Central Bilbao isn't too large and is reasonably walkable. The Guggenheim museum, as far afield as many people get, is about 20 minutes' walk from the old town along the river. For further-flung parts of Bilbao, such as the beach or the bus station, the metro is excellent. Sir Norman Foster's design is simple, attractive and, above all, spacious. Although there's a reasonable network of local bus services in Bilbao, they are only generally useful for a handful of destinations; these are indicated in the text. The tram network is handy, particularly for reaching the Guggenheim from the old town. There's just one line so far; a scenic one, running from Atxuri station along the river, skirting the Casco Viejo (stopping behind the Teatro Arriaga), then continuing on the other side of the Nervión, stopping at the Guggenheim and the bus station among other places.

Tip...

If you're planning to be in the city for a few days it's worth picking up the **Bilbao Bizkaia Card** (www.bilbao bizkaiacard.com), which allows free transport on local buses, metro, tram and the Artxanda funicular, as well as free entry to most of the city's museums and tourist attractions, shopping discounts and entrance to many attractions around the province. It costs €30 for a day, €35 for two days, or €40 for three days and is available from the tourist office.

Best pintxo bars
El Globo, page 51
Gatz, page 52
Gure Toki, page 52
La Viña del Ensanche, page 52

Best places to stay
Gran Domine Bilbao, page 47
Hotel Sirimiri, page 48
Iturrienea Ostatua, page 48
Hotel Embarcadero, page 49

When to go

Bilbao's summers are warm but not baking. This is the best time to visit, but be sure to book ahead during the boisterous August fiesta (see Festivals, page 55). At other times of year, Bilbao is a fairly wet place, but never gets especially cold. The bar life and museums provide ample distraction from the drizzle.

Time required

At least three days to see the main sights.

Weather Bilbao/Bilbo

January 14°C / 6°C / 71mm	**February** 14°C / 6°C / 67mm	**March** 16°C / 8°C / 71mm
April 17°C / 8°C / 109mm	**May** 20°C / 11°C / 87mm	**June** 22°C / 14°C / 55mm
July 24°C / 16°C / 50mm	**August** 24°C / 17°C / 60mm	**September** 23°C / 14°C / 91mm
October 20°C / 13°C / 105mm	**November** 16°C / 9°C / 136mm	**December** 14°C / 7°C / 96mm

Bilbao's old town is a good place to start exploring the city. This is where most of the budget accommodation and bar life is based. Tucked into a bend in the river, it's the most charming part of town, a lively jumble of pedestrian streets that has always been the city's social focus. There's something of the medina about it; on your first few forays you surely won't end up where you might have thought you were going.

Siete Calles

The parallel Siete Calles (seven streets) are the oldest part of town, and even locals struggle to sort out which bar is on which street. While there aren't a huge number of sights per se, there are dozens of quirky shops and some very attractive architecture; leisurely wandering is in order. The true soul of the Casco emerges from early evening on, however, when Bilbaínos descend like bees returning to the hive, strolling the streets, listening to buskers, debating the quality of the *pintxos* in the myriad bars and sipping wine in the setting sun.

Catedral de Santiago

In the centre of the old town area is the **Catedral de Santiago** ⓘ *Mon-Sat 1100-1300, 1700-1930, Sun 1100-1330, free*, whose slender spire rises high above the tight streets. A graceful Gothic affair, it was mostly built in the late 14th century on the site of a previous church, but was devastated by fire in the 1500s and lost much of its original character. Two of its best features are later additions: an arched southern porch and a small but harmonious cloister (if it's locked, ask an attendant). The interior is small and has an inclusive, democratic air. Also worth spotting is a beautifully worked Gothic tomb in the chapel of San Antón. Promoted to cathedral in 1950, the building has benefited from restoration work. A few shops are charmingly nestled into its flank.

Plaza Nueva

The 'New Square', one of a series of similar cloister-like squares in Euskadi, was finished in 1849. Described by Unamuno (see box, page 42) as "my cold and uniform Plaza Nueva", it will particularly appeal to lovers of geometry and symmetry with its courtly neoclassical arches, which conceal an excellent selection of restaurants and bars, offering some of the best *pintxos* in town. In good weather, most have seating outside in the square.

> **Tip...**
>
> *Pintxos*, the Basque version of tapas, are big business in Bilbao, and no trip would be complete without going on a *txikiteo* (*pintxo* crawl). Hit the Casco Viejo for traditional canapé-style *pintxos*, or the Ensanche for cooked-to-order gourmet bites.

Museo Vasco

Near the Plaza Nueva, the **Euskal Museoa/Museo Vasco** ⓘ *Plaza Miguel de Unamuno 4, T944 155 423, www.euskal-museoa.org, Mon and Wed-Fri 1000-1900, Sat 1000-1330, 1600-1900, Sun 1000-1400, €3 (free on Thu)*, is attractively set around an old Jesuit college and houses an interesting if higgledy-piggledy series of Basque artefacts and exhibits covering thousands of years. There's a fascinating room-sized relief model of Vizcaya on the top floor, a piece of one of the Gernika oak trees and some good displays on Basque fishing. Across the square and up the steps, the **Museo Arqueológico** ⓘ *Calzadas de Mallona 2, T944 040 990, Tue-Sat 1000-1400, 1600-1930, Sun 1030-1400, €3*, has a well-presented overview of Vizcaya's prehistory and history through material finds. Most of the prehistoric artefacts were found in caves around the province.

Arenal and around

Formerly an area of marshy sand, the Arenal was drained in the 18th century. It is now a busy nexus point for strollers, lovers, demonstrators and dog walkers, and has a bandstand with frequent performances, often of folk dancing. Next to it is the 18th-century baroque façade of **San Nicolás de Bari**. Opposite, the **Teatro Arriaga** seems very sure of itself these days, but was only reopened in 1986 after decades of neglect. It's very much in plush *fin de siècle* theatre style, with chandeliers, soft carpet and sweeping staircases, but at times presents some fairly cutting-edge art, usually of a high standard and fairly priced.

Essential País Vasco

Getting around

Excellent transport connections throughout the region mean a hire car's not a necessity. Bilbao airport has many flights, including budget connections.

Time required

Seven to 10 days.

When to go

There's plenty of precipitation, mostly drizzle, from autumn to spring, but good and not-too-hot summers. Prices on the coast are sky-high in August, but Bilbao is affordable year-round.

Basílica de Begoña

Atop a steep hill above the Casco Viejo, the Basílica de Begoña is Bilbao's most important church, home of the Virgin of Begoña, the patron of Vizcaya. It's built in Gothic style on the site of a chapel where the Virgin is said to have appeared in former times. The cloister is a later addition, as is the flamboyant tower, which gives a slightly unbalanced feel to the building. To get there from the Casco Viejo, take the lift from Calle Esperanza or leave the Casco Viejo metro station by the 'Begoña/Mallona' exit. From there, walk up the hill to the basilica. Buses No 3 and No 30 come here from Plaza Circular, or bus No 41 from Gran Vía. On your way back down, rather than taking the Mallona lift, head down the flight of stairs next to it; a charming descent into the Casco Viejo warren, emerging on Plaza Unamuno.

Along the riverbank

derelict industrial area reinvented as a cultural precinct and social space

"You are, Nervión, the history of the town, you are her past and her future, you are memory always becoming hope." Miguel de Unamuno.

The **Nervión** river made Bilbao and Bilbao almost killed the Nervión; until recently pollution levels were sky-high. Although your immune system would still have words to say about taking a dip, the change is noticeable. The riverbank has been and continues to be the focus of most of Bilbao's beautification schemes.

Cross the river at the **Zubizuri** footbridge, one of the most graceful of the acclaimed bridges of Santiago Calatrava. After crossing the footbridge, you are on the

Bilbao/Bilbo

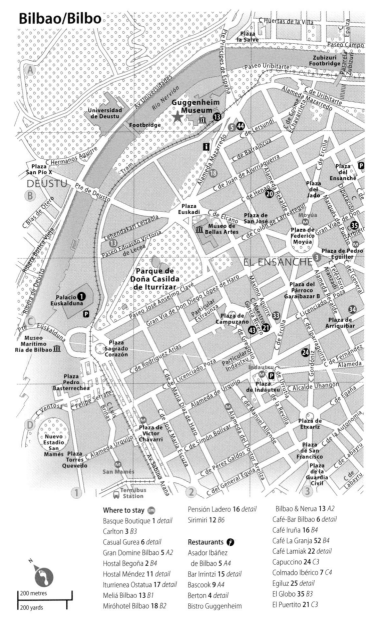

Where to stay 🏨
Basque Boutique **1** *detail*
Carlton **3** *B3*
Casual Gurea **6** *detail*
Gran Domine Bilbao **5** *A2*
Hostal Begoña **2** *B4*
Hostal Méndez **11** *detail*
Iturrienea Ostatua **17** *detail*
Meliá Bilbao **13** *B1*
Miróhotel Bilbao **18** *B2*
Pensión Ladero **16** *detail*
Sirimiri **12** *B6*

Restaurants 🍴
Asador Ibáñez
de Bilbao **5** *A4*
Bar Irrintzi **15** *detail*
Bascook **9** *A4*
Berton **4** *detail*
Bistro Guggenheim

Bilbao & Nerua **13** *A2*
Café-Bar Bilbao **6** *detail*
Café Iruña **16** *B4*
Café La Granja **52** *B4*
Café Lamiak **22** *detail*
Capuccino **24** *C3*
Colmado Ibérico **7** *C4*
Egiluz **25** *detail*
El Globo **35** *B3*
El Puertito **21** *C3*

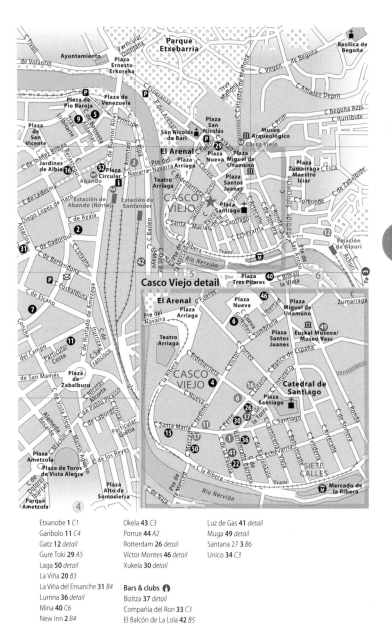

Etxanobe **1** *C1*	Okela **43** *C3*	Luz de Gas **41** *detail*
Garibolo **11** *C4*	Porrue **44** *A2*	Muga **49** *detail*
Gatz **12** *detail*	Rotterdam **26** *detail*	Santana 27 **3** *B6*
Gure Toki **29** *A5*	Víctor Montes **46** *detail*	Unico **34** *C3*
Laga **50** *detail*	Xukela **30** *detail*	
La Viña **20** *B3*		
La Viña del Ensanche **31** *B4*	**Bars & clubs** 🍸	
Lurrina **36** *detail*	Bizitza **37** *detail*	
Mina **40** *C6*	Compañía del Ron **33** *C3*	
New Inn **2** *B4*	El Balcón de La Lola **42** *B5*	

BACKGROUND
Bilbao

In 1300 the lord of the province of Vizcaya, Don Diego López de Haro V, saw the potential of the riverside fishing village of Bilbao and granted it permission to become a town. The people graciously accepted, and by the end of the 14th century history records that the town had three parallel streets: Somera, Artekale and Tendería. These were soon added to: Belostikale, Carnicería Vieja, Barrenkale and Barrenkale Barrena, forming the Siete Calles – the seven original streets of the city. It was a time of much strife and the fledgling town was walled, but at the end of the 15th century these original fortifications came down and the city began to grow.

Bilbao suffered during the first Carlist war in the 19th century, when the liberal city was besieged (ultimately unsuccessfully) by the reactionary Carlist forces. The one bright spot to emerge was the invention of *bacalao al pil-pil*, now the city's signature dish, but originally devised due to lack of any fresh produce to eat. Not long after the war, Bilbao's boom started. The Vizcayan hills harboured huge reserves of haematite, the ore from which the city's iron was produced. By the middle of the century, it had become evident that this was by far the best ore for the new process of steelmaking. Massive foreign investment followed, particularly from Britain, and the city expanded rapidly as workers flooded in from all parts of the peninsula. The good times didn't last, however, and by the early 20th century things were looking grimmer. Output declined and dissatisfied workers sank into poverty. The Civil War hit the city hard too; after the Republican surrender, Franco made it clear he wasn't prepared to forgive the Basques for siding against him. Repressed and impoverished, the great industrial success story of the late 19th century fell into gloom.

The dictator's death sparked a massive reflowering of Basque culture, symbolized by the bold steps taken to revitalize the city. The Guggenheim's opening in 1997 confirmed Bilbao as a cultural capital of Northern Spain, and ongoing regeneration works proceed apace.

Paseo Uribitarte; this riverside walk leading to the Guggenheim museum is where plenty of Bilbaínos gather for the evening stroll.

The tram is another good way to see the river, running more or less along it from Atxuri station to the Guggenheim and Euskalduna palace.

★ Museo Guggenheim
Abandoibarra Etorbidea 2, T944 359 000, www.guggenheim-bilbao.es, Tue-Sun 1000-2000 (Jul and Aug daily 1000-2000), €13, students/pensioners €7.50, children under 12 free, €16 including Museo de Bellas Artes; guided tours free at 1230 (daily in English), 1700 (Tue to Sat in Spanish, Sun in Basque). The closest metro stop to the museum is Moyúa, but it's a few blocks away; better is the tram, which stops just outside.

Daring in concept and brilliant in execution, the Guggenheim museum has driven a boom in the local confidence as well as, more prosaically, the economy; its success gave the green light to further ambitious transformations of the formerly industrialized parts of the city.

It all started when the Guggenheim Foundation decided to build a new museum to enable more of their collection to be exhibited. Many cities around the globe were considered, but Bilbao was keenest and the Basque government was prepared to foot the US$100 million bill for its construction.

Frank Gehry was the man who won the design competition and the rest is the reality of what confronts visitors to Bilbao today: a shining temple of a building that completely fulfils the maxim of 'architecture as art'. Gehry's masterstroke was to use titanium, an expensive soft metal normally reserved for Boeing aircraft and the like. He was intrigued by its futuristic sheen and malleable qualities; the panels are literally paper-thin. The titanium makes the building shimmer: it seems that the architect has managed to capture motion.

One of the most impressive features of the design is the way it interacts with the city. One of Bilbao's enjoyable and surprising experiences is to look up when crossing a street in the centre of town and see the Guggenheim perfectly framed, like some unearthly craft that's just landed. Gehry had to contend with the ugly bulk of the Puente de la Salve running through the middle of his site, yet managed to incorporate the bridge fluidly into his plans. The raised tower at the museum's eastern end has no architectural purpose other than to link the building more effectively with the town upriver; it works.

The building also interacts fluidly with the river itself; the pool at the museum's feet almost seems part of the Nervión, and Fuyiko Nakaya's mist sculpture, when turned on, further blurs things. It's entitled *FOG*, which also happen to be the architect's initials. The same pool also hosts Yves Klein's Fire Fountain pyrotechnics.

A couple of creatures have escaped the confines of the gallery and sit in the open air. Jeff Koons's giant floral sculpture, *Puppy*, sits eagerly greeting visitors. Formerly a touring attraction visiting the city for the opening of the museum in 1997, he couldn't escape the clutches of the kitsch-hungry Bilbaínos, who demanded that he stayed put. On the other side of the building, a sinister spider-like creature guards the waterside approach. Entitled *Maman*, we can only be thankful that late sculptor Louise Bourgeois's mother had long since passed away when it was created. It's a striking piece of work, and makes a bizarre sight if approached when the mist is on. More comforting are Koons's colourful bunch of *Tulips* by the pool under the gallery's eaves.

So much for the exterior, which has met with worldwide acclaim. What about the inside? It is, after all, an art museum. Gehry's idea was that there would be two types of gallery within the building: "galleries for dead artists, which have classical square or rectangular shapes, and galleries for living artists, which have funny shapes, because they can fight back". The embodiment of the latter is the massive Gallery 104, built with the realization that many modern artworks are too big for traditional museums. This has been dedicated to Richard Serra's magnificent *The Matter of Time*, an installation now consisting of eight monumental structures of curved oxidized steel centered around *Snake*, whose curved sheets will carry whispers from one end to another. A hundred feet long, and weighing 180 tons, it's meant to be interactive – walk through it, talk through it, touch it. Other pieces, including one that's disturbingly maze-like, play with space, angles, and perception in different ways. Off the gallery is an interpretative exhibition on the pieces.

This, however, is one of only a few pieces that live in the museum; the rest are temporary visitors, some taken from the permanent collection of the Guggenheim Foundation, others appearing in a range of exhibitions. This, of course, means that the overall quality varies according to what's on show.

Tip...
If you only take one stroll in Bilbao, an evening *paseo* from the Casco Viejo along the river to the Guggenheim should be it.

BACKGROUND
ETA and Basque nationalism

Although many Spaniards refuse to distinguish between the two, Basque nationalism and terrorism are two very different things. The vast majority of Basque nationalists, ie those who want more autonomy or complete independence for the region, are firmly committed to a peaceful and democratic path. ETA, on the other hand, were traditionally pessimistic about the possibility of achieving these aims in this manner, and sought by planned violent action to force the issue.

To probe the wrongs, rights and history of the issue would require volumes. Viewed in the context of a changing Europe, Basques have a strong case for independence, being culturally and ethnically distinct to Spaniards. The real sticking point is that Spain has no intention of giving up such a profitable part of the nation. Economics don't permit it, old-fashioned Spanish honour doesn't permit it and, cleverly, the constitution doesn't permit it. It isn't likely to happen, and most Basques know it. From this frustration a small percentage of extremism developed.

The nationalist movement was born in the late 19th century, fathered by Sabino Arana, a perceptive but unpleasant bigot who was a master of propaganda. He devised the *ikurriña* (the Basque flag), coined terms such as *Euskadi*, and published manifestos for independence, peppered with dubious historical interpretations.

The tragically short-lived breakthrough came with the Civil War. The sundered Republic granted the Basques extensive self-government, and José Antonio Aguirre was installed as *lehendakari* (leader) at Gernika on 7 October 1936. A young, intelligent and noble figure, Aguirre pledged Basque support to the struggle against Fascism. The government was forced into exile a few months later when the Nationalists took Bilbao, but Basques fought on in Spain and later in France against the Nazis.

The birth of ETA can be directly linked to the betrayal of the Basque government by the western democracies. At the end of the Second World War, supporters of the Republic had hoped that a liberating invasion of Spain might ensue. It didn't, but Franco's government was ostracized by the USA and Europe. The Basque government in exile was recognized as legitimate by the western powers. However, with the Cold War chilling up, the USA began to see the value of the anti-communist Franco, and granted a massive aid package to him. Following suit, France and Britain shamefully cosied up the fascist government and withdrew support from the horrified Basques.

ETA was founded by angry Basque youth shortly after this sordid political turnabout. Its original goal was simply to promote Basque culture in repressive Spain, but it soon took on a violent edge. In 1959 it adopted the name, which stands for Euskadi Ta Askatasuna, The Basque Country and Freedom. They conducted their first assassination in 1968, and over the years were responsible for over 800 deaths,

Architecturally, the interior is a very soothing space, with natural light flooding into the atrium. It's a relief to realize that this isn't one of those galleries that makes you feel you'll never be able to see everything unless you rush about; it's very uncluttered and manageable. In the atrium is Jenny Holzer's accurately titled *Installation for Bilbao*, an arresting nine-column LED display that unites the different levels of the building.

mostly planned targets such as politicians, Basque 'collaborators' and police. The organization was primarily youthful, and used extortion and donations to fund its activities. Their main demands were, in line with those of many nationalists, autonomy for the Basque region and the union of Navarra with the region, as well as hopefully the French Basque region. Their logo features a snake, representing politics, wrapped around an axe, representing violence, with the motto *Bietan jarrai* (Keep up on both).

Despite the slogans, there was nothing noble or honourable about ETA's normal modus operandi. In many cases it seems that the central leadership had little control over its trigger-happy thugs, and many targets were people with families with little or no power within the regime. The attitude of the international public turned against ETA after their glory days; in 1973, when Franco's right-hand man Admiral Carrero Blanco was sent sky-high by an ETA bomb, the terrorist group were liberationist heroes to many.

For many years, the government and police were in a vicious and self-defeating cycle of violence with ETA. Whenever the terrorist group struck, their support dropped dramatically in Euskadi. A few days later, when a mystery retaliatory killing of Basques occurred, anti-government feeling would rise again.

The escalationist attitude of the Madrid government continued in 2002, when the parliament overwhelmingly passed legislation specifically designed to ban Batasuna, the political party often (and probably accurately) linked with ETA. The party was then banned by the courts, outraging Basques and their governing PNV (no friends of Batasuna) as well as many international observers. During the same period, the police embarked on a massive operation, with many high-profile arrests and discovery of arms caches. This significantly impacted the group, as did changing attitudes in the wake of 9/11 and the Madrid train bombings. The 2004 election promised much, as José Luis Rodríguez Zapatero initially favoured dialogue with ETA, despite the right's condemnation of "dealing with terrorists". ETA declared a ceasefire in 2006, but broke it, and stepped up their bombings and assassinations in 2008 in response to a major government crackdown. A continuing 'judicial offensive', with several Basque organizations and political parties banned by the courts, dovetailed with the police operations and left ETA, whose support within the Basque lands had dramatically dwindled, looking increasingly weak and anachronistic.

The Basque region has a high degree of autonomy, and a high standard of living, and many Basques were heartily sick of the group's mafia-like extortion. In 2010 they announced another ceasefire, and, in late 2011, Zapatero's handling of the problem seemed finally vindicated when the group announced a permanent cessation of armed activity. At time of writing, this was holding, and there was a genuine feeling that the violence, and ETA as we knew it, might finally have come to an end.

The effect created is a torrent of primal human sentiment expressed simply in three languages. Nearby are Jim Dine's towering but headless *Three Red Spanish Venuses*.

There are three floors of galleries devoted to temporary exhibitions radiating off the central space. For a look at some smaller-scale Frank Gehry work, drop into the reading room on the ground floor, furnished with his unusual cardboard chairs and tables, which

BACKGROUND
The philosopher's last stand

One of Bilbao's most famous sons was Miguel de Unamuno, poet, philosopher and academic, born in 1864 on Calle Ronda. A member of the 'Generation of '98' – a new wave of artists and thinkers emerging in the wake of the Spanish-American war of 1898 – Unamuno, who spoke 15 languages, was a humanist and a Catholic with an idealistic love of truth. This made him enemies in a Spain where political beliefs tended to come first. To this day, many Basques have mixed feelings about 'Don Miguel', who, although proud of being Basque, wasn't pro-independence and deplored some of the myths created in the name of nationalism.

Unamuno became rector of the university at Salamanca but after criticizing the dictatorship of Primo de Rivera, he was imprisoned in the Canary Islands, from where his rescue was organized by the editor of the French newspaper *Le Quotidien*.

In Salamanca when the Civil War broke out, Unamuno, previously a deputy in the Republic, had supported the rising, but grew more and more alarmed with the nature of the Nationalist movement and the character of the war. On 12 October, 1936 he was presiding over the Columbus day ceremony at the university. The gathering degenerated into a fascist propaganda session. Catalan nationalism was denounced as a cancer that fascism would cut out, and General Millán Astray, a war veteran, continued with more empty rhetoric; the hall resounded to the popular Falangist slogan "Viva la muerte", or "long live death".

Unamuno rose to close the meeting: "At times to be silent is to lie", he said, and went on to criticize harshly what had been said. The general responded by crying "Death to intellectuals". Guns were pointed at the 72-year-old, who continued: "You will win, because you have the brute force. But you will not convince. For to convince, you would need what you lack: reason and right in the struggle". At the end of his speech, he was ushered out of the tumultuous hall by Franco's wife to safety. Under house arrest, he died a couple of months later, it was said, of a broken heart. On the day of his death, his two sons enlisted in the anti-fascist militia.

are surprisingly comfortable and solid. The cafés also feature chairs designed by him. As well as the usual gallery shop, the museum also has an excellent modern art bookshop.

There's a spot in the museum designed to display Picasso's *Gernika*, which the Basque government persistently tries to prize away from the Reina Sofía gallery in Madrid.

Palacio Euskalduna

Beyond the Guggenheim, the Euskalduna Palace is a bizarre modern building that echoes both the shipbuilding industry and Vizcaya's iron trade. It's now a major venue for conferences and concerts, particularly classical. More *simpático* is the covered Euskalduna bridge nearby, which sweeps into Deustu in a confident curve.

Museo Marítimo Ría de Bilbao

Muelle Ramón de la Sota 1, T946 085 500, www.museomaritimobilbao.org, Tue-Fri 1000-1800 (2000 summer), Sat and Sun 1000-2000, €6 (extra applies for special exhibitions), free Tue.

This museum nestles under the Euskalduna bridge and examines the maritime history of this proud city. It's on the site of what was once an important shipbuilding and cargo area; a massive derrick and various ships in dry dock are part of the exterior exhibition. Inside, the focus is on the Bilbao estuary and Vizcayan shipping in general. It's dry but fascinating, with a couple of good audiovisual presentations in English (other displays have translation sheets). One of the highlights is the aerial photograph of Bilbao and its *ría*. There are often excellent temporary exhibitions, which have included visiting 'guest ships' that moor outside.

Deustu

traditional student area with great local character

Across from the Guggenheim is Deustu, a bohemian university district buzzing with purpose. Sometimes dubbed 'The Republic of Deustu', it developed separately from Bilbao for much of its history and still has a different vibe. Traditionally frequented by artists, students and agitators, the cafés and bars hum with political discussion. If you want that perfect snap of Frank Gehry's masterpiece, this is the place to come, particularly in the evening light.

The Universidad de Deustu, Bilbao's main university, was founded in 1886 by the Jesuits. It now counts over 20,000 students and staff among its several buildings. While the academic standard of the university has traditionally been very high, it was an important centre of radical opposition to the Franco dictatorship, and has also played a major role in Basque nationalism.

On Deustu's waterfront, a large sculptured stone feline defies the sky. This building was originally a pavilion to house the small workshops of local tradespeople but has now been converted into luxury apartments. Bilbaínos call it **El Tigre** (the tiger), but the city is divided; many agree that it's actually a lioness.

El Ensanche

the modern centre with a great art gallery and top eating options

The residents of old Bilbao had long been crammed into the small Casco Viejo area when the boom came and the population began to surge. In 1876 the Plan de Ensanche (expansion) de Bilbao was approved, and the area across the river was drawn up into segments governed by the curve of the Nervión. The Ensanche quickly became Bilbao's business district, and it remains so today, its graceful avenues lined with stately buildings, prestigious shops and numerous bars.

Museo de Bellas Artes

Plaza del Museo 2, T944 396 060, www.museobilbao.com, Metro Moyúa, Wed-Mon 1000-2000, €7, free Wed, €16 with Guggenheim, €3 audio guide.

Not to be outdone by its titanium colleague, the fine arts museum has tried to keep up with the times by adding a modern building of its own on to the existing museum. The result is a harmonious credit to its architect, Luis Uriarte, who seamlessly and attractively fused new to old. Similarly, the collection is a medley of modern (mostly Basque) art and older works – there's also a new space for temporary exhibitions.

Athletic Bilbao

Rarely is a football team loved quite as deeply as Athletic Club are by Bilbao. A Basque symbol in the same league as the *ikurriña* or the Gernika oak, the team, as a matter of principle, only fields Basque players. Astonishingly they have remained competitive in one of the strongest leagues in the world and have never been relegated. To date, they have won the championship eight times (more than any other club bar the two Madrid giants and Barcelona) and have won 23 Spanish Cups.

Athletic Club grew out of the cultural exchange that was taking place in the late 19th century between Bilbao and the UK. British workers brought football to Bilbao, and Basques went to Britain to study engineering. In the early years, Athletic fielded many British players, and their strip was modelled on that of Sunderland, where many of the miners were from. José Antonio Aguirre, who led the Civil War Basque government so nobly, had been a popular player up front for the club.

The Basque sculptors Eduardo Chillida and Jorge de Oteiza (see box, page 66) are both well represented, but the museum confidently displays more avant-garde multimedia work by young artists too. Among the portraits, the jutting jaw of the Habsburg kings is visible in two famous works. The first, of a young Felipe II, is by the Dutchman Moro, while the Felipe IV, attributed to Velázquez, and similar to his portrait of the same king in the Prado, is a master work. The decline of Spain can be seen in the sad king's haunted but intelligent eyes, which seem to follow the viewer around the room. A lighter note is perhaps unintentionally struck by the anonymous *Temptations of St Anthony*, who is pestered by a trio of colourful demons. Among other items of interest is a painting of Bilbao by Paret y Alcázar. Dating from 1793 and painted from the Arenal, it looks like a sleepy riverside village. Here too, is a very good modern restaurant upstairs offering great views.

Plaza de Toros de Vista Alegre
Check the website, www.plazatorosbilbao.com, for details of corridas and ticketing.

Bilbao's temple of bullfighting sees most action during **Semana Grande** in August, when there are *corridas* all week. The locals are knowledgeable and demanding of their matadors, and the bulls they face are acknowledged to be among the most *bravo* in Spain. Tickets to the spectacles start at about €15. The bullring is also home to a **museum** ⓘ *C Martín Agüero 1, T944 448 698, Metro Indautxu, Mar-Oct Mon-Fri 1000-1330, 1600-1800, Nov-Feb Mon-Fri 1000-1330, €3*, dedicated to tauromachy. There are displays on the history of the practice, as well as memorabilia of famous matadors and bulls.

Estadio de San Mamés
Plaza Pedro Basterrechea, Metro San Mamés, T944 411 445, www.athletic-club.net.

The new Estadio de San Mamés, opened in 2013 next to the old one, is at the far, western end of the new town. Few in the world are the football teams with the social and political significance of Athletic Bilbao (see box, above); support of the team is a religion, and this, their home stadium, is known as the Cathedral of Football. Services are held fortnightly. The Basque crowd are fervent but good-natured. It's well worth going to a game; it's a far more friendly and social scene than the average match in the rest of Europe. The Monday papers frequently devote 10 pages or more to Athletic's game. Tickets usually go on sale at the ground two days before the game but may be available online by the time you read this. On match days, the ticket office opens two hours before kick-off. Tickets range from €25-50 depending on location. The new ground will also hold a **museum**, still under construction at time of last research, displaying trophies and other memorabilia of 'Los Leones'. Entry will include a guided tour of the stadium.

Bilbao's seafront

some of the Basque Country's best beaches within a Metro ride of the city

At the mouth of the estuary of the Nervión, around 20 km from Bilbao, the fashionable barrio of Getxo is linked by the improbably massive Puente Vizcaya with the grittier town of Portugalete, in its day a flourishing medieval port. It's a great day trip from Bilbao; the fresh air here is a treat for tired lungs, and not far from Getxo stretch the languid beach suburbs of Sopelana, Plentzia and Gorliz.

Getxo

Very much a separate town rather than a suburb of Bilbao, Getxo is a wealthy, sprawling district encompassing the eastern side of the river mouth, a couple of beaches, a modern marina, and a petite old harbour. It's home to a good set of attractive stately mansions as well as a tiny but oh-so-pretty whitewashed old village around the now disused fishing port-ette. There's a very relaxed feel about the place, perhaps born from a combination of the seaside air and a lack of anxiety about where the next meal is coming from.

Playa de Ereaga The Playa de Ereaga is Getxo's principal stretch of sand, and location of its **tourist office** ⓘ *T944 910 800, www.getxo.net/turismo*, and finer hotels. Near it, the **Puerto Viejo** is a tiny harbour, now silted up, and a reminder of the days when Getxo made its living from fish. The solemn statues of a fisherman and a *sardinera* stand on the stairs that look over it, perhaps mystified at the lack of boats. Perching above, a densely packed knot of white houses and narrow lanes gives the little village a very Mediterranean feel – unless the *sirimiri*, the Bilbao drizzle, has put in an appearance. There are a couple of restaurants and bars to soak up the ambience of this area, which is Getxo's prettiest quarter.

Playa de Arrigunaga Further around, the Playa de Arrigunaga is a better beach flanked by crumbly cliffs, one topped by a windmill, which some days has a better time of it than the shivering bathers. A pleasant, if longish, walk leads downhill to the estuary end of Getxo, past the marina, and an ostentatious series of 20th-century *palacios* on the waterfront, and a monument to Churruca, whose engineering made the estuary navigable, making Bilbao accessible to large vessels; a vital step in its growth.

Passing the hulking modern **Iglesia de Nuestra Señora de las Mercedes** (which contains some highly regarded frescoes) will bring you to the unmistakable form of the Puente Bizkaia and the trendy shopping area of **Las Arenas** (Areeta).

Puente Bizkaia

www.puente-colgante.com, 1000-2200 crossings, 1000-dusk walkway; crossings €0.40 per person, €1.55 per car; walkway €7, Metro Areeta or Portugalete.

A bizarre cross between a bridge and a ferry, the World Heritage Puente Bizkaia was opened in 1893, a time when large steel structures were à la mode in Europe. Wanting to connect

ON THE ROAD

La Pasionaria

"It is better to be the widow of a hero than the wife of a coward." Dolores Ibárruri.

One of the most prominent figures of the Spanish Civil War, Dolores Ibárruri, from the Bilbao suburb of Gallarta, near Portugalete, was known as La Pasionaria (the passion flower) for her inspirational public speaking.

Formerly a servant and a *sardinera* (sardine seller), she suffered grinding poverty and the loss of two daughters in infancy, but rose to prominence in the Communist Party in the 1930s, becoming a deputy in the parliament in 1936 (she was released from prison to take up her post). When the Civil War broke out, she became a powerful symbol of the defence of Madrid and the struggle against fascism as well as empowered womanhood. Straightforward, determined and always dressed in black, she adopted the war cry *"No pasarán"* (they shall not pass), which was taken up all over Republican Spain. She was instrumental in the recruitment and morale of anti-fascist soldiers, including the International Brigades. When the latter were withdrawn, she famously thanked them: "You can go proudly. You are history. You are legend … We shall not forget you". Ibárruri was never much involved in the plotting and infighting that plagued the Republican cause and was able to claim at the end of the war: "I have neither blood nor gold upon my hands". When Franco was victorious in 1939, she flew to Russia, where she lived in Moscow. The dictator died in 1975 and, after 38 years, Ibárruri was re-elected to her old seat at the first elections in 1977. On her return to Spain the 82-year-old Pasionaria, still in black, proclaimed to a massive crowd: "I said they shall not pass, and they haven't". She died in 1989.

the estuary towns of Getxo and Portugalete by road, but not wanting a bridge that would block the *ría* to shipping, the solution taken was to use a 'gondola' suspended by cables from a high steel span. It's a fascinating piece of engineering: the modern gondola fairly zooms back and forth with six cars plus foot passengers aboard. You can also ascend to the walkway 50 m above. The bridge is often referred to as the **Puente Colgante** (hanging bridge).

Portugalete

On the other side of the Puente Bizkaia from Getxo is Portugalete, a solid working-class seamen's town with a significant seafaring history. In former times, before Churruca did his channelling work, the Nervión estuary was a silty minefield of shoals, meanders and sandbars – a nightmare to navigate in anything larger than a rowing boat. Thus Bilbao was still a good few hours' journey by boat, and Portugalete's situation at the mouth of the *ría* gave it great importance as a port. Nowadays, although from across the water it looks thoroughly functional, it preserves a characterful old town and attractive waterfront promenade.

Above the waterside the old Casco is dominated by the **Basílica de Santa María**, commissioned by Doña María 'the Kind' at the time of the town's beginnings, although the current building, in Gothic style, dates from the early 16th century. There's a small museum inside. Next to it, the **Torre de Salazar** is what remains of the formidable compound built by Ochoa de Salazar, a major landowner, in about 1380. The main living area was originally on the second floor – the first was a prison – and the tower was occupied until 1934, when a fire evicted the last residents. A member of the Salazar family who lived here, Lope García, was one of the first chroniclers of Vizcaya. He had plenty of time to devote to his writings, as he spent the last few years of his life locked up by his loving sons.

West of Portugalete, in Galdames, the **Torre Loizaga** ① *T946 802 976, www.torreloizaga. com, Sun and public holidays 1000-1500, €10*, is a picturesque tower whose owner has one of the world's finest collections of Rolls-Royces and other luxury cars.

Beaches beyond

Beyond Getxo, **Sopelana** has picturesque cliffs bracketing three excellent beaches. Get here on the Metro from Bilbao to Larrabasterra.

Further on, **Gorliz** is a coastal settlement sheltered in a pretty shell-shaped bay. The beach is great, with protected water ideal for windsurfing and family-friendly swimming. The Metro stop Plentzia is a stroll away.

Inland from Plentzia, in **Gatika**, the unusual Castillo de Butrón was transformed from a medieval fort into an extravagant neo-Gothic fairtytale castle by the 19th-century lord that owned it. It's surrounded by lush gardens. At time of writing, you could only wander around the exterior, pending restoration works.

Listings Bilbao/Bilbo *map page 36.*

Tourist information

The tourist offices can provide a good free map of the city; they can also sell you the **Bilbao Bizkaia Card** (see page 33). Make sure you also pick up a copy of the excellent bi-monthly tourist magazine *Bilbao Guía*. The city's website, www.bilbaoturismo.net, is also a good source of information. The tourist board runs an accommodation and event-booking website, www.bilbaohoteles. com, T902 877 298. As well as those listed below, there is a tourist office at the airport.

Bilbao tourist office
Pl Circular 1, T944 795 760, www.bilbao.net. Daily 0900-2100.
The city's main tourist office is an excellent source of information.

Museo Guggenheim tourist office
Alameda Mazarredo 66. Sep-Jun Mon-Sat 1000-1900, Sun 1000-1500, Jul-Aug daily 1000-1900.
A small but handy place for information.

Portugalete tourist office
La Canilla Ibilbidea, T944 729 314, www.portugalete.com.

Where to stay

Finding accommodation is frequently difficult; it's worth phoning ahead, although some of the *pensiones* won't take reservations. Most budget accommodation is in or near the Casco Viejo, while the classier hotels are spread through the new town.

€€€€ Gran Domine Bilbao
Alameda Mazarredo 61, T944 253 300, www.hoteldominebilbao.com.
This modern 5-star hotel is directly opposite the Guggenheim and has been designed with the same innovation and levity in mind. The original façade of the building consists of 48 mirrors at slightly different angles, while the delightful interior is dominated by a large central atrium. The rooms with Guggenheim views cost a little more, but it's worth it when you're paying prices of this level (though online discounts are plentiful outside peak times). There's also a good bar and restaurant. Inspiringly original. Recommended.

€€€ Hotel Carlton
Plaza Moyúa 2, T944 162 200, www.hotelcarlton.es.

This grand old hotel, set on noisy Plaza Moyúa, is considerably more luxurious inside than out. Its refurbished neoclassical ambience has colonnaded Einstein, Lorca and Hemingway, among other notables. Rooms are spacious, and there are some good deals online.

€€€ Meliá Bilbao
Lehendakari Leizaola Kalea 29, T944 280 000, www.melia.com.
Another impressive addition to Bilbao's collection of modern and monumental buildings around this part of town, this striking reddish giant is just a short stroll from the Guggenheim and the Museo de Bellas Artes. Excellent modern rooms feature really stylish bathrooms and are chock-full of facilities like electronic window blinds. There's a good restaurant and a major shopping centre opposite.

€€€ Miróhotel Bilbao
Alameda Mazarredo 77, T946 611 880, www.mirohotelbilbao.com.
Also close to the Guggenheim, with some great views of it, this is a sleek hotel with a Catalan touch; both architect Carmen Abad and interior designer Antonio Miró hail from Barcelona. It's impressively modern, with a pared-back feel not without touches of whimsy. The rooms are excellent: spacious and with a Nordic feel to the white fittings. Rates vary substantially according to when you reserve; you may get better deals from an online broker than the hotel's own website. There are all services, including an enjoyable jacuzzi and a stylish bar. Staff are helpful and friendly.

€€ Basque Boutique
C de la Torre 2, T944 134 849, www.basqueboutique.es.
Up some stairs in a venerable building with no lift, this lovely staffless boutique *pensión* surprises with its charmingly offbeat decor, comfortable rooms and buzzy feel. You're in the heart of the tapas zone, so there's some noise at night.

€€ Casual Gurea
C Bidebarrieta 14, T944 163 299, www.casualhoteles.com.
Carefully refurbished and well-scrubbed friendly establishment on one of the Casco Viejo's principal axes. Rooms are all en suite, modern and comfortable if by no means luxurious. Though it advertises itself as a hotel these days, it still feels more like a boutique *pensión*.

€€ Hostal Begoña
C Amistad 2, T944 230 134, www.actioturis.com.
Very handy for the train station and Casco Viejo, this is a welcoming modern *hostal* offering good comfort. From the inviting library/lounge to the large chalet-style rooms and mini-suites at very reasonable prices, this is an excellent option.

€€ Hotel Sirimiri
Plaza de la Encarnación 3, T944 330 759, www.hotelsirimiri.com.
Named after the light misty rain that is a feature of the city, this is a small gem of a hotel in a quiet square a short stroll from the Casco Viejo. The genial owner has equipped it with a gym and sauna, and there's limited free parking – a big saving – at the back. Rooms come with heating but not a/c. The twins are much more spacious than some of the doubles. Follow signs for Miraflores/Atxuri from the motorway and it's very easily reached.

€€ Iturrienea Ostatua
C Santa María 14, T944 161 500, www.iturrieneaostatua.com.
This beautiful *pensión* in the heart of the Casco Viejo *pintxo* zone is carefully lined in stone, wood, art, and idiosyncratic objects. With delicious breakfasts (extra) and homely rooms, you might want to move in. Recommended.

€ Hostal Méndez
C Santa María 13, T944 160 364, www.pensionmendez.com.
A dignified building with castle-sized doors and an entrance guarded by iron dogs. The

1st floor has *hostal*-grade rooms with new bathrooms, while the 4th floor is *pensión*-style accommodation, simpler, but still very adequate. Many rooms have balconies, but there's street noise until midnight or later.

€ Pensión Ladero
C Lotería 1, T944 150 932, www.pensionladero.es.
Right in the thick of it, this welcoming option has cork tiles, good shared bathrooms and very low-priced rooms with TV, some of which are reached by a tiny spiral staircase. There's some echoing noise but you'll receive a hearty Basque welcome – just as well, as it's on the 4th floor with no lift. Excellent value and the price doesn't change by season. Recommended. No bookings taken.

Bilbao's seafront
Staying here is a good alternative to the city; there are plenty of options.

€€€ Hotel Embarcadero
Av Zugazarte 51, T944 803 100, www.hotelembarcadero.com, Metro Areeta.
With an excellent seafront location, this grand old villa now houses an excellent boutique hotel. The spacious, attractive rooms come with modern flowery wallpaper; pay the little extra for a wide water view. Recommended.

€€€-€€ Gran Hotel Puente Colgante
C María Díaz de Haro 2, T944 014 800, www.granhotelpuentecolgante.com. Euskotren Portugalete, Metro Areeta.
A reconstructed 19th-century building with a grand façade, this upmarket modern hotel is superbly situated next to the Puente Bizkaia on the waterfront promenade. All rooms face outwards, and the hotel has all the facilities you need. There are good discounted rates available via the website.

€€ Hotel Artaza
Av Los Chopos 12, T944 912 852, www.hotelartaza.com, Metro: Neguri.
This lovely sandstone palace in Getxo offers a comfortable elegance and easy access to the water. It's got an appropriately old-fashioned feel and has a great garden and terraced café-restaurant.

Bilbao's Casco Viejo is undoubtedly the prime place to head for *pintxos* and evening drinking, with the best areas being the Plaza Nueva and around the Siete Calles, with a particularly earthy and vibrant Basque scene at the top of C Somera. There's another concentration of bars on Av Licenciado Poza and the smaller C García Rivero off it. The narrow C Ledesma, a street back from Gran Vía, is a popular place to head for lunch set menus or after-work snacks and drinks. There are some good restaurants in the Casco Viejo (including several geared solely to tourists), but also plenty of options scattered through the New Town and Deustu. While you'll see the cold *pintxos* arrayed before you in most bars, some of the best snacking options are the ones they cook to order – have a look for a menu or chalkboard listing what they are.

€€€ Asador Ibáñez de Bilbao
C Ibáñez de Bilbao 6, T944 233 034, www.asadoribanezdebilbao.com.
This smart spot is a traditional meat restaurant specializing in roast lamb, which emerges from the kitchen in enormous chunks on traditional clay dishes and beautifully tender. Service is polite and there's also a good variety of fresh shellfish and crustaceans if the meat sounds a bit much.

€€€ Bistró Guggenheim Bilbao
Av Abandoibarra 2, T944 239 333, www.bistroguggenheimbilbao.com.
The Guggenheim, since it opened, has always endeavoured to provide quality eating experiences alongside the art. This bistro is excellent, striking just the right note between gourmet and casual eating. The dining room offers great river views and an excellent set menu for €29.50. The café out front is a good bet for a snack and a drink under the portico too. There's also

In the Basque Country, from about 1900 in the evening until midnight or so, everyone lives in the street, walking, talking, drinking and eating *pintxos*.

Wherever you go in the region, you'll be confronted and tempted by a massive array of food across the top of bars. Many bars serve up very traditional fare: slices of tortilla (potato omelette) or *pulgas de jamón* (small rolls with cured ham). Other bars, enthused by 'new Basque' cuisine, take things further and dedicate large parts of their day to creating miniature food sculptures using more esoteric ingredients. The key factor is that they're all meant to be eaten. Many places will prepare hot *pintxos* straight from the kitchen – these have to be ordered but are always well worth the short wait and are usually the highlight of a bar's repertoire. For the cold ones atop the bar, you can ask the bartender or usually simply help yourself to what you fancy, making sure to remember what you've had (or keep the toothpicks) for the final reckoning. If you can't tell what something is, ask: ¿de qué es?. *Pintxos* usually cost between €1.50 and €3.50 depending on the bar and ingredients.

a gourmet restaurant, **€€€ Nerua**, www. neruaguggenheimbilbao.com, T944 000 430, on site, which offers an ultra-minimalist dining room and 3 elaborate tasting menus (€105 to €175) featuring beautiful morsels created using molecular techniques and excellent quality produce.

€€€ Etxanobe
Abandoibarra Etorbidea 4, T944 421 071, www.etxanobe.com.
On the top floor of the hulking Euskalduna conference centre, this gourmet restaurant does lots right in its exquisite tasting menu which encompasses both forage and molecular philosophies as well as the Basque obsession with quality ingredients. The atmosphere is friendlier than in many similar gastronomic temples.

€€€ Mina
Muelle Manzana s/n, T944 795 938, www.restaurantemina.es.
Rated by many Bilbao foodies as the most enjoyable place to eat in town, this restaurant faces the Casco Viejo on the riverbank. Expect creative combinations that you haven't seen before and are unlikely to again. There's no menu, but the *table d'hôte* is excellent and beats more pretentious places that charge twice the price. Service is top notch. Recommended.

€€€ Porrue
Alameda Rekalde 4, T944 231 313, www.porrue.com.
Perfectly placed for a post-Guggenheim special meal, this intimate, romantic space is decorated with contemporary flair, with mood – almost nightclub – lighting and numerous whimsical touches. The cuisine focuses on seasonal ingredients and the service is caring. One of the city's best. Recommended.

€€€ Víctor Montes
Plaza Nueva 8, T944 157 067, www.victormontes.com.
This traditional and excellent restaurant is known for its huge collection of wines and whiskies. The elegant upstairs dining room has the best of Basque cuisine at surprisingly reasonable prices. Downstairs is a very popular *pintxo* bar; if you can shoulder your way to it in the evening, you'll find that not a square inch is free of posh and delicious bites.

€€ Bascook
C Barroeta Aldamar 8, T944 009 977, www.bascook.com.

This attractive, romantic basement space run by an innovative young chef makes a great change from the *pintxo* scene. The menu features Asian fusion, Basque and vegetarian dishes, and the flavour combinations are great. Mon-Fri lunchtimes you can pick 2 dishes from the menu with dessert for €30 – a top deal, but it's compassionately priced in any event.

€€ Colmado Ibérico
Alameda Urquijo 20, T944 436 001,
www.colmadoiberico.com.
A feast of piggy products, this welcoming locale is both a ham shop and a bar/restaurant, where you can munch on a basic (but delicious) *pulga* of Spain's finest ham or more elaborate pork-based creations.

€€ Egiluz
C Perro 4, T944 150 242,
www.restauranteegiluz.com.
Among all the bright modern lights of the Casco Viejo's newer restaurants, this sturdy old family-run place is still the place to go if you fancy a steak or similar. The dining room is upstairs at the back of the bar. They serve a huge *chuletón* – it could comfortably feed 2 – and other excellent grilled and roasted fare.

€€ La Viña
C Henao 27, T944 243 602, Metro Moyúa.
You could easily miss this tiny bar wedged into a block in the Ensanche. As well as being a hospitable place to have a glass of wine, they serve some very fine food at a very fair price. Their speciality is seafood, with mussels, crabs, or whatever's fresh to choose from and eat at the handful of small tables.

€ Capuccino
C Gordóniz 2, T944 436 980,
www.cafecapuccinoylacanela.com.
A place for people in the know. This café, run by a friendly Egyptian, and with a map of the old Nile painted on the roof, serves filled pitta rolls, as well as *shawarma*, musaka, and other snacks. They have an excellent range of teas.

€ Garibolo
C Fernández del Campo 7, T944 223 255,
www.garibolo.com, Metro Moyúa.
Opens for lunch Mon-Sat.
There are now a few vegetarian restaurants in Bilbao, but this, the original, is still the best. The colourful Garibolo packs 'em in for its good value lunches. No alcohol served.

€ Laga
C Merced 2, T944 164 770.
This bright, simply decorated bar is one of the Casco's best places for simple, no-nonsense wholesome Basque food. Particularly recommended are the croquettes, but it's all good, including the fresh fish, the garlicky steaks and the *mollejas* (sweetbreads). Great value.

€ Rotterdam
C Perro 6, T944 162 165.
Small, uncomplicated Casco Viejo restaurant with a *simpático* boss. This is what lunch restaurants have always been like here, with a cheap, uncomplicated *menú del día*.

Pintxo bars

€€ Berton
C Jardines 11, T944 167 035.
The hanging *jamones* and bunches of grapes define this cheerful bar, which has top-notch ham *pintxos* and *raciones* and some quality wines by the glass. It's mushroomed in recent years, and now has another bar around the corner and one opposite. All offer better value for tapas at the bar than sit-down meals.

€€ Café-Bar Bilbao
Plaza Nueva 6, T944 151 671,
www.bilbao-cafebar.com.
A sparky place with top service and a selection of some of the better gourmet *pintxos* (all labelled) to be had around the old town. It's always busy, but the bar staff never seem to miss a trick.

€€ El Globo
C Diputación 8, T944 154 221,
www.bardetapasbilbao.com.

There's an extraordinary variety of cold and cooked-to-order hot *pintxos* at this compact place near the Moyúa square. Traditional bites take their place alongside wildly imaginative modern creations. The hot *foie pintxos*, lightly dusted with fresh-ground black pepper, are to kill for. Outstanding. Recommended.

€€ El Puertito
Corner of García Rivero and Licenciado Poza, T944 026 254, www.elpuertito.es.
On this fertile *pintxo* street in the Ensanche, this is a top little place to perk up your palate with toothsome fresh-shucked oysters from a variety of Spanish and other European cold-water coasts (€1-3 per oyster), accompanied by an ice-cold dry white. Delicious.

€€ Gatz
C Santa María 10, T944 154 861, www.bargatz.com.
A convivial bar with warm, non-designer decor and some of the Casco's better *pintxos*, which are frequent contenders in the awards for such things. Happily spills on to the street at weekends. Friendly, no-nonsense staff. Recommended.

€€ Gure Toki
Plaza Nueva 12, T944 158 037, www.guretoki.com.
In a corner of the square, this tight-packed bar offers a good range of elaborate bartop and cooked-to-order hot *pintxos* and a convivial atmosphere.

€€ La Viña del Ensanche
C Diputación 10, T944 155 615, www.lavinadelensanche.com.
This historic central spot is where you'll find Bilbao execs escaping from the office for a quick *pintxo*. Great ham and *bonito* are on offer, as well as tasty little hot stews. Service is good, and there are delicious wines available by the glass. There's a tablet with English translations if you're struggling. Like what you taste? Take it home from the shop next door.

€€ Lurrina
Barrenkale Barrena 16, T944 163 277, www.lurrina.com.
This old-town bar shines out onto the historic street with its cheery light and modern blond wood. It opens later than most in this zone, and is always a good option with its tasty *pintxo* combinations, outdoor seating and upbeat staff.

€€ Okela
C García Rivero 8, T944 415 937, www.barokela.com.
A modern bar popular with the office crowd and dominated by a huge signed photo of the footballer Joseba Etxebarría in full stride for Athletic Bilbao. Decent *pintxos*. There are several other good choices on this street.

€€ Xukela
C Perro 2, T944 159 772, www.facebook.com/xukela.
A very social bar on a very social street. Attractive *pintxos* and some good sit-down food – cheeses and cured meats – and a clientele upending glasses of Rioja at a competitive pace.

€ Bar Irrintzi
C Santa María 8, T944 167 616, www.irrintzi.es.
With a vibe so laid-back that there's not even a till: the takings are under colour-coordinated bottles behind the counter, this Casco Viejo bar doesn't skimp on the quality. *Pintxos* are an art form, with a superb array of imaginative snacks, all carefully labelled, freshly made and delicious.

Cafés

Café Iruña
Jardines de Albia s/n, T944 237 021, www.cafeirunabilbao.net.
This noble old establishment on the Jardines de Albia has begun its 2nd century in style and is more popular than ever, with people spilling out onto the street. Well refurbished, the large building is divided into a smarter café/restaurant space with wood panelling

in neo-Moorish style, and a tiled bar with old sherry ads and some good *pintxos* – including lamb kebabs sizzling on the grill in the corner.

Café La Granja
Plaza Circular 3, T944 230 813, www.cafelagranja.net.
A spacious old Bilbao café, opened in 1926. Its high ceilings and long bar are designed to cope with the lively throng that gathers throughout the day. Attractive art nouveau fittings and *pintxos*, with tasty croquettes, rolls and focaccias, and a corner bar dedicated to making mojitos.

Café Lamiak
C Pelota 8, T944 159 642.
A peaceful and likeable 2-floor forum, the sort of place a literary genre, pressure group or world-famous band might start out. It's a mixed gay/straight crowd, with a relaxed atmosphere.

New Inn
Alameda Urquijo 9, T944 151 043.
The restored art nouveau splendour of the main bar of this popular café is reason enough to enter. It's a great breakfast option, with a succulent range of flavoured tortillas.

Bilbao's seafront
There's plenty of good eating in these waterside suburbs.

€€€ Asador El Puerto/Zabala
C Aretxondo 20, Getxo, T944 912 166, www.puertozabala.com, Metro Algorta.
With fresh seafood right off the boats and a great location by Getxo's old port, this makes a prime fish-eating destination. There's no menu: they just tell you what's fresh that day. Prices can add up, but the quality shines through.

€€€ Cubita
Ctra Galea 30, Getxo, T944 911 700, www. restaurantecubita.com, Metro Bidezabal.
A highly acclaimed restaurant with a great location by the windmill above Arrigunaga

beach. The beautifully elegant interior oversees the freshest of seafood brought out from the acclaimed young chef's kitchen.

€€ Karola Etxea
C Aretxondo 22, Getxo, T944 600 868, www.karolaetxea.net, Metro Algorta.
Perfectly situated in a quiet lane above the old port. It's a good, not too expensive place to try some fish; there are usually a few available, such as *txitxarro* (scad) or *besugo* (sea bream). The *kokotxas* (cheeks and throats of hake in sauce) are also delicious.

€ El Hule
C Victor Chavarri 13, Portugalete, T944 722 104.
In the narrow, sloping streets of Portugalete's old town (just behind the town hall on the waterfront near the Puente Colgante), this is a cracking spot for lunch. The small but cute upstairs and downstairs dining rooms are cosy and comfortable. The food is traditional, uncomplicated fare served with a smile and plenty of quality.

Bars and clubs

Bilbao's nightlife is very quiet during the week, but it makes up for it at weekends. Most bars have to shut at 0400 these days, but there are some *discotecas* that go later. Nearly everywhere in the Casco Viejo shuts by 0130, but you can always dash across the Puente de la Merced to the streets around C Hernani, where there is plenty going on. Be careful in this zone though, as muggings are not unknown. There are lots of bars in the Casco Viejo, including many on the legendary streets of Ronda, Somera and Barrenkale, the latter famous for its boisterous rock 'n' roll scene.

Bars

Bizitza
C Torre 1, T944 165 882.
Very chilled mixed gay-straight bar with a Basque political slant. Relaxed, atmospheric and welcoming, with frequent cultural events. One of the top spots for an after-

dinner *copa* in Bilbao – they mix a great drink. Recommended.

Compañía del Ron
C Máximo Aguirre 23, T944 213 069, www. laciadelron.com. Closes early, around 2300.
Friends of Ronald will be happy here, with hundreds of rums at the disposal of the bar staff, who know how to handle them. As well as the ones you can drink, there's quite a collection out the back to browse. Recommended.

Luz de Gas
C Pelota 6, T944 790 823.
A beautiful mood bar with an oriental touch. Sophisticated but friendly, and you can challenge all-comers to chess or Connect-4.

Muga
C María Muñoz 8, T944 162 781, www.muga.blogia.com.
A long-time favourite, this relaxed café and bar has a rock 'n' roll vibe, with colourful tables, fanzines and CDs for sale, and a down-to-earth clientele. There's also vegan and vegetarian burgers and the like available.

Clubs

El Balcón de La Lola
C Bailén 10, www.facebook.com/ balcondelalola. Open latish; concerts earlier in the night.
Decorated in industrial style with sheet-metal and graffiti, this is a weekend-opening club that varies in character from fairly cheesy dance to pretty heavy garage. Mixed.

Santana 27
C Tellería 27, Bolueta, T944 598 617, www. santana27.com. Open nightly 2300-0600.
Near the metro station in Bolueta, this vast venue has opened out here to avoid the strict opening hours in central Bilbao. There are often concerts and other events; the nightclub section, **Fever** (www.fever.es) has

so many dance floors that you are bound to find something you like; it often has live bands and special club nights. Usually €5-10 to get in, including a drink.

Unico
Alameda Urquijo 30, T944 158 338, www.facebook.com/unicobilbao.
Packed from about 0200 on Fri and Sat nights. The music is fairly light *bakalao*, the crowd mixed and good-looking, the drinks horrendously expensive, but entry is usually free.

Entertainment

Music venues
Bilbo Rock, *Muelle de la Merced s/n, T944 151 306, www.bilbao.net/bilborock*. Atmospheric venue in a converted church that is now a temple of live rock with bands playing most nights of the week. No licence, but canned beer from machines.
Kafe Antzokia, *C San Vicente 2, T944 244 625, www.kafeantzokia.eus*. An ex-cinema turned Bilbao icon, this is a live venue for anything from death metal to Euskara poetry, and features 2 spacious floors with bars which go late and loud at weekends. Sociable, friendly, and a place where you might hear more Euskara than Spanish.
Palacio Euskalduna, *C Abandoibarra 4, T944 310 310, www.euskalduna.eus*. Top-quality classical performances from the symphonic orchestras of Bilbao and Euskadi, as well as high-profile Spanish and international artists.

Theatre
Teatro Arriaga, *Plaza Arriaga 1, T944 792 036, www.teatroarriaga.com*. Bilbao's highest-profile theatre is picquesely set on the river by the Casco Viejo. It's a plush treat of a place in late 19th-century style, but the work it presents can be very innovative. The better seats go for €30 and above, but there are often decent pews available for around €10.

The best-known Basque sport is **pelota**, www.euskalpilota.com, sometimes called *jai alai*, played on a three-sided court known as a *frontón*. In the most common version, two teams of two hit the ball with their hands against the walls seeking, like squash, to prevent the other team from returning it. The ball is far from soft; after a long career players' hands resemble winning entries in a root-vegetable show. Variations of the game are *pelota a pala*, using bats, and *cesta punta*, using a wickerwork glove that can propel the ball at frightening speeds. Most courts have matches on Saturday and Sunday evenings. Confusingly, the seasons vary from town to town, but there's always something on somewhere. Bilbao's Bizkaia court (www.bizkaiafrontoia.com), on the southern edge of the city, is the biggest venue in the region. Other traditional Basque sports tend to be unreconstructed tests of strength, such as **wood-chopping**, or the alarming **stone-lifting**, in which stocky *harrijasotzaileak* dead-lift weights in excess of 300 kg. The best places to see these sports are at village fiestas.

Festivals

Early Jul BBK Live, www.bilbaobbklive.com. This major music festival brings big-name pop and rock acts to the city over 3 days.
Sat after 15 Aug Aste Nagusia (big week), Bilbao's major fiesta, follows on from those in Vitoria and San Sebastián to make a month of riotous Basque partying. It is a boisterous mixture of everything: concerts all over town, *corridas*, traditional Basque sports and serious drinking. If you're a light sleeper, make sure you book a hotel out of earshot from the live music stages – Madrid is a good bet.

Shopping

Bilbao is the best place to shop in Northern Spain. The majority of mainstream Spanish and international clothing stores are in the Ensanche, particularly on and around C Ercilla. The Casco Viejo harbours dozens of quirkier shops. A commercial centre, **Zubiarte**, just by the Puente de Deustu, has a full complement of fashion chains and a cinema.

Mercado de la Ribera, the art deco market by the river where stallholders used to come for the weekly market, has over 400 stalls selling fruit, veg, meat and fish; it's the major centre for fresh produce in Bilbao.

Come in the morning if you want to get the true flavour; afternoons are comparatively quiet. There's also a bar/restaurant here with regular live music and tasty food.

There are numerous great delis for buying Basque and Spanish produce; **Txorierri**, in the old town at Artekale 19, is one, **Oka**, at Marqués del Puerto 1 near Plaza Moyúa, is another.

What to do

Basque Taste, T697 884 520, *www.basque taste.com*. Offer various food- and wine-oriented tours, as well as visits focusing on the city's architecture or on the Guggenheim itself. Tours run on foot or by bike and are very entertaining. Recommended.
Bilbao Paso a Paso, T944 730 078, *www. bilbaopasoapaso.com*. Knowledgeable tours of Bilbao and the whole of Euskadi that can be tailored to suit.
Bilboats, T644 442 055, *www.bilboats.com*. Boat trips along the Nervión. The basic €12 jaunt takes you up past the Guggenheim – have the cameras ready – but the longer €18 trip takes you right up the estuary to the sea, past the ghosts of the city's industrial past.
Bus Turistikoa, *www.busturistikoa.com*. This double-decker bus runs around the city

stopping 15 times in the standard hop-on, hop-off circuit. A 24-hr ticket is €14.
Instituto Hemingway, *C Bailén 5, T944 167 901, www.institutohemingway.com.* Language school.

Bilbao's seafront

Getxo is a base for a whole range of activities, from diving to horse riding and, especially, sailing. There are lots of operators; the best first point of contact is the helpful **tourist office**, T944 910 800, www.getxo.net/en/turismo.

Transport

Bilbao's airport is a good gateway to Northern Spain with connections to several European destinations. The Portsmouth–Bilbao ferry service is another appealing option. The city is well served by buses from the rest of the nation and is exceedingly well connected with Vitoria, San Sebastián and smaller destinations in Euskadi. There are a few train services to other Spanish cities and a narrow-gauge line along the coast to Santander, Oviedo and Galicia.

Air

Bilbao's airport near **Sondika/Loiu**, 10 km northeast of the centre, is a beautiful building designed by Santiago Calatrava, seemingly in homage to the whale. A taxi to/from town costs about €20-25. There's an efficient bus service that runs to/from Bilbao's bus station via Plaza Moyúa in central Bilbao. It leaves from outside the terminal, takes 20-30 mins and runs every half hour. One-way €1.45.

Bicycle hire

Alquimoto, *C Anselma de Salces 9, T944 012 563, www.alquimoto.com,* rent bikes, scooters and motorbikes, though they're quite a way from the centre. **Tourné**, *C Villarías 1, T944 249 465, www.tourne bilbao.com. Daily 1000-2000.* Handily located on the riverfront opposite the

Arenal, this outfit rents out bikes for €8/15/20 per half/full day/24 hrs. They also have tandems available.

Boat

Brittany Ferries, *T0871 244 0744, www. brittany-ferries.co.uk.* Connect Bilbao with Portsmouth 1-2 times weekly. The ferries leave from a terminal at Zierbena, 21 km from the centre of Bilbao. The closest metro stop is Santurzi, 3 km away, from where it's a short ride in a cab.

Bus

The majority of Bilbao's inter-urban buses leave from the Termibus station near the football stadium (Metro San Mamés, tram stops outside). All long-haul destinations are served from here, but several Basque towns are served from the stops next to Abando station on C Hurtado Amezaga.

To **San Sebastián**: buses from the Termibus station every 30 mins weekdays, every hour at weekends, operated by **PESA** (1 hr 20 mins). To **Vitoria**: buses from the Termibus station about every 30 mins with **Autobuses La Unión** (55 mins). Other destinations include **Santander** (almost hourly, 1 hr 30 mins), **Pamplona** (7-9 daily, 2 hrs), **Logroño** (5 daily, 2 hrs), and **Burgos** (4 direct daily, 2 hrs).

Car

Though the centre is fairly well signposted, the 1-way system and extensive pedestrianization can make it difficult to find your way around. Parking in the centre is metered; if your hotel doesn't have private parking, you're best off in one of the underground car parks, which cost around €15-25 for 24 hrs. The handiest for the Casco Viejo is **Arenal**; cross the Puente del Ayuntamiento from the new town and turn right. When approaching Bilbao by road from the east, it's worth paying the small toll through the Artxanda tunnel, which brings you in to town right alongside the

Guggenheim museum, saving much time and potential to get lost.

Car hire The usual assortment of multinationals dominate. The process is fairly painless, and national driving licences are accepted. **Atesa**, C Sabino Arana 9, T944 423 290; Aeropuerto de Bilbao, T944 533 340, www.atesa.es; **Avis**, Av Doctor Areilza 34, T944 275 760; Aeropuerto de Bilbao, T944 869 648, www.avis.com; **Hertz**, C Doctor Achucarro 10, T944 153 677; Aeropuerto de Bilbao, T944 530 931, www.hertz.com.

Metro
Bilbao's metro (www.metrobilbao.eus) runs Sun-Thu until about 2400, Fri until about 0200, and 24 hrs on Sat. A single fare costs from €1.50, while a day pass is €4.60. There's 1 main line running through the city and out to the beach suburbs, while the 2nd line heads out to the coast on the other side of the estuary.

Train
Bilbao has 3 train stations. The main one, **Abando**, is the terminal of **RENFE**, the national Spanish railway. It's far from a busy network but it's the principal mainline service. There are 2 direct trains daily to **Madrid** (5 hrs) and other connections via Zaragoza. 2 trains daily go to **Barcelona** (6¾ hrs).

Abando is also the main terminus for **Euskotren**, www.euskotren.eus, a handy short-haul train network that connects Bilbao and San Sebastián with many of the smaller Basque towns as well as their own outlying suburbs. The other Bilbao base for these trains is **Atxuri**, situated just east of the Casco Viejo, an attractive but run-down station for lines running eastwards as far as San Sebastián. These are particularly useful for reaching the towns of Euskadi's coast. **Gernika** is serviced every hour and on to **Mundaka** and **Bermeo**. Trains to **San Sebastián** run every hour on

the hour (2 hrs 40 mins) via **Zarautz**, **Zumaia**, **Eibar**, and **Durango**.

Narrow-gauge **FEVE** trains connect Bilbao along the coast to **Santander**, 3 times daily (2½ hrs) and beyond. They are slow but scenic and leave from the Estación de Santander just next to Bilbao's main Abando railway station. There's also a daily service from here to **León** (7 hrs 15 mins).

Tram
A single costs €1.50 (€4.70 for a day ticket); there are machines at the tram stops. It runs every 10-15 mins or so. You have to validate your ticket in the machine on the platform before boarding.

Getxo
Bus
Buses No 3411 and No 3413 run to/from **Plaza Moyúa** every 30 mins.

Metro
Getxo is a large area, and the metro stations Areeta, Gobela, Neguri, Aiboa, Algorta, and Bidezabal all fall within it. The beaches further on can be accessed from Larrabasterra, Sopelana and Plentzia metros.

Portugalete
Bus
Bus No 3152 from the Arenal bus station in Bilbao (Mon-Sat).

Metro
Bilbao's Metro (Line 2) now runs to Portugalete; the Line 1 station of Areeta is also handy, just across the Puente Colgante.

Train
From Abando station, the **Euskotren** service runs to Portugalete (line: Santurtzi) every 12 mins weekdays, less frequently at weekends, and takes 20 mins.

Basque
Region

San Sebastián/
Donostia

★ The sweep of La Concha bay and the hills overlooking it draw comparisons for San Sebastián, a 2016 European Capital of Culture, with Rio de Janeiro. One of the peninsula's most beautiful cities with a superb natural setting, lovely sandy beaches, and a regular influx of international stardom during its film festival, it's a relaxed and enjoyable place that has been invigorated by the addition of two excellent museums and a piece of world-class modern architecture in the Kursaal auditorium. It's also the gourmet capital of Spain, whether you splash out on sumptuous degustation menus or graze elaborate *pintxos*. Its eating scene is quite extraordinary, and has to be seen to be believed.

The pedestrianized Old Town lies at the foot of the Monte Urgull hill, and is unabashedly devoted to tapas bars; the *pintxos* here are astoundingly inventive, small works of art in their own right. The bars are in constant competition to take gourmet cuisine one step further. From the old town, the main beach stretches west right around the bay to picturesque Monte Igueldo. The hills behind town are green and studded with villages that seem totally oblivious to the city's presence. This is where cider is made: in spring people descend like locusts on the cider houses to drink it straight from the vat and eat enormous meals over sawdust floors. It's amazing any cider's left to be bottled.

The liveliest part of San Sebastián is its old section at the eastern end of the bay. Although most of it was destroyed by the 1813 fire, it is still full of character, with a dense concentration of *pintxo* bars, *pensiones*, restaurants and shops. Protecting the narrow streets is the solid bulk of Monte Urgull, which also shelters the small harbour area.

El Muelle

One of the city's loveliest meanders is along Paseo Nuevo, which runs around the hill from the river mouth to the harbour. Beyond the town hall, San Sebastián's small fishing and recreational harbour, El Muelle, is a pleasant place to stroll around. There's a handful of cafés and tourist shops, and you can see the fishermen working on their boats while their wives mend the nets by the water. Halfway round the harbour is a monument to 'Aita Mari' (father Mari), the nickname of a local boatman who became a hero for his fearless acts of rescue of other sailors in fierce storms off the coast. In 1866 he perished in view of thousands attempting yet another rescue in a terrible tempest.

The **Museo Naval** ⓘ *Paseo del Muelle 24, T943 430 051, www.untzimuseoa.net, Tue-Sat 1000-1400, 1600-1900, Sun 1100-1400, €3, free Thu*, is a harbourside museum, which unfortunately makes a potentially intriguing subject slightly dry and lifeless. While there's plenty of information about Basque seafaring, the interesting aspects are hurried over

Essential San Sebastián/Donostia

Finding your feet

San Sebastián's airport is at Hondarribia, 20 km east of the city (see page 80). San Sebastián's main **RENFE** terminus is the Estación del Norte just across the river from the new town area. Next to it is the new Donostia bus station. Also, regular buses leave to and from Plaza Guipúzcoa and the surrounding streets to other nearby destinations in the province. The city itself is reasonably compact and most sights are within easy walking distance of each other. Buses run from one end of the city to the other.

Best pensiones

Pensión Aída, page 72
Pensión Altair, page 72
Pensión Amaiur, page 72
Pensión Kursaal, page 72

Best places to eat

Arzak, page 74
Zuberoa, page 74
Casa Urola, page 74
Borda Berri, page 75
Casa Gandarias, page 75
La Cuchara de San Telmo, page 76

When to go

The city is packed out in July and August with hotel prices among the most expensive in Spain and the beach packed with upmarket sunseekers.

Time required

Two to three days.

and there's little attempt to engage the visitor. Descriptions are in Spanish and Euskara only, though there is a printed leaflet with some English info.

At the end of the harbour, San Sebastián's **aquarium** ⓘ *Plaza Carlos Blasco de Imaz s/n, T943 440 099, www.aquariumss.com, Tue-Thu 1000-1900 (2000 in summer), Fri-Sun 1000-2000 (2100 in summer), €13 (€6.50 for kids)*, is well stocked. The highlight is a tank brimming with fish, turtles, rays and a couple of portly sharks to keep the rest of them honest. There's a perspex tunnel through the tank, which can be viewed from above. Unfortunately, there's not much in the way of identification panels and viewing space can get crowded, particularly around shark-feeding time (Tuesday-Sunday at 1200), which isn't quite as dramatic as it sounds. Most fascinating are the shark egg cases, in which you can observe the tiny embryos. There is a bar/restaurant and shop on site.

Monte Urgull

The bulk of Monte Urgull is one of several Donostia spots that you can climb up to appreciate the view. An important defensive position until the city walls were taken down in 1863, it saw action from the 12th century onwards in several battles. The hill is topped by a small fort, the **Castillo de la Mota** ⓘ *daily summer 1100-1330, 1700-2000, Oct-Apr Thu-Fri 1000-1400, 1500-1730, Sat-Sun 1000-1730*, once used as the residence of the town's *alcalde* and as a prison. It has a small collection of old weapons, including a sword that belonged to the last Moorish king Boabdil. There's also a large statue of Christ, the **Monumento al Sagrado Corazón**, adding to San Sebastián's credentials as a Rio lookalike.

Motorboats to Isla Santa Clara in the middle of the bay leave from Monte Urgull, as do boats offering cruises round the harbour.

Basílica de Santa María del Coro

In the heart of the old town, and with a façade about as ornate as Spanish baroque ever got, the church of Santa María del Coro squats under the rocks of Monte Urgull and faces the newer cathedral across the city. After the exuberant exterior, the interior is a contrast of low lighting, heavy oil paintings and incense. Above the altar is a large depiction of the man the city was named after, unkindly known by some as the 'pincushion saint' for the painful way he was martyred. Facing him at the other end of the nave is a stone crucifix in the unmistakable style of Eduardo Chillida, the Basque sculptor (see box, page 66).

Museo San Telmo ① *Pl Zuloaga 1, T943 481 580, www.santelmomuseoa.com, Tue-Sun 1000-2000, €6, children free, Tue free.* This stunningly refurbished museum skillfully blends old – a 16th-century Dominican convent with perfect Renaissance cloister – and new architecture. There are excellent temporary exhibitions on the ground floor, as well as an impressive audiovisual in the church. Upstairs is an exhibition on the growth and industrialization of the Basque Country in the 19th and 20th centuries, and on the top floor is a good collection of art. Fittingly, as the museum sits on a square named after him, Ignacio Zuloaga is well represented. A worthy successor to the likes of Velázquez and Goya in the art of portrait painting, one of the best examples here is his *Columbus*, who is deep and soulful (and suspiciously Basque-looking). There's also a small memorial to Zuloaga in the plaza outside.

Iglesia de San Vicente

The most interesting of San Sebastián's churches, San Vicente is a castle-like sandstone building that squats in the northeast of Parte Vieja. Started in the early 16th century, it features a massive *retablo* with various biblical scenes, and a gallery with an impressive organ. Jorge Oteiza's wonderfully fluid, modern *Pietà* stands outside the southern door.

La Bretxa

This modern complex lies at the point where the besieging English and Spanish forces entered the city during the Peninsular War – the name means 'the breach'. The main attraction is the underground food market, with fish, in particular, of spectacular quality.

Centro and New Town

one of Europe best city beaches but don't expect to have it to yourself

Playa de la Concha

This beautiful curving strip of sand, has made San Sebastián what it is. Named La Concha (shell) for its shape, it gets seriously crowded in summer but is relatively quiet at other times, when the chilly water makes swimming a matter of bravado. Behind the beach, and even more emblematic, is the **Paseo Miraconcha**, a promenade barely changed from the golden age of seaside resorts. It's still the place to take the sea air and is backed by gardens, a lovely old merry-go-round, and a row of desirable beachfront hotels and residences that still yearn for the days when royalty strolled the shore every summer season.

Isla Santa Clara

Out in the bay this is a pretty rocky island that could have been placed there purposely as a feature. There's nothing on it but a lighthouse and a jetty, but it's prime picnic territory and the setting is unbeatable. It's only accessible by public transport during the summer, when a motorboat leaves from the harbour close to the end of the beach.

Ondarreta

Where the beach of La Concha graciously concedes defeat at a small rocky outcrop, the beach of Ondarreta begins. This is a good place to stay in summer, with less hustle and bustle. Atop the rock sits the **Palacio de Miramar**; commissioned by the regent María Cristina in the late 19th century, it would not look out of place offering bed and breakfast in an English village.

The **beach** of Ondarreta gazes serenely across at the rest of San Sebastián from beyond the Palacio de Miramar. It's a fairly exclusive and genteel part of town, appropriately watched over by a statue of a very regal Queen María Cristina. The beach itself feels

San Sebastián/Donostia

Ⓐ

Monumento al
Sagrado Corazón

Museo
Naval

Aquarium

El Peine
del Viento

Isla
Santa Clara

To...

Ⓑ Funicular

**Monte
Igueldo**

Plazoleta
Funicular

Bahía de la Concha

Jardines de Ondarreta

Playa de
Ondarreta

Av Satrústegui

Ⓒ

ONDARRETA

C. Pamplona-Iruña

Playa de
la Concha

Paseo Miraconcha

Plaza
Alfonso XIII

Palacio de
Miramar

Calle Escolta Real

Paseo Duque de Baena

Paseo de la P...

Av Zumalacárregui

C. María

Parque
Zubimusu

35

Paseo Pío Baroja

Paseo
de Barojo

1

2

3

San Sebastián detail

Museo de
San Telmo

Santa María
del Coro

San Vicente

C 31 de Agosto

de Bilbao

Inglo

Euskal Herria

12

6

4

Plaza
Constitución

36

28

Puerto

Calbetón

25

7

24

23

32

Mercado
de la
Bretxa

C Gral
Etxague

29

15

C R Regente

P

Mayor

Esterlines

C San Lorenzo

9

M

Pl Kanpandegui

Narrika

Juan de Bilbao

Iñigo

Embeltrán

13

i

Teatro Victoria
Eugenia

5

Bilbo

Igentea

Ayuntamiento

C Hernani

C Elcano

Alameda del
Boulevard

C Garibay

Bengoetxea

Oquendo

N

200 metres
200 yards

Where to stay 🛌
Camping Igueldo **15** *B1*
De Londres y
 de Inglaterra **3** *B4*
Izar Bat **7** *detail*
María Cristina **12** *B5*
Pensión Aída **5** *B6*
Pensión Altair **17** *A6*
Pensión Amaiur **6** *detail*

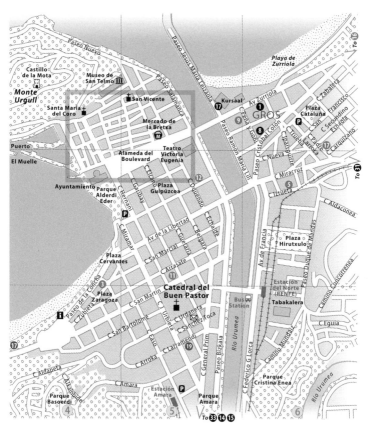

Pensión Gran Bahía
  Bernardo **13** *detail*
Pensión Kursaal **9** *A5*
Pensión San Lorenzo
  10 *detail*
Pensión San Martín **11** *B5*
Villa Soro **16** *A6*

Restaurants
A Fuego Negro **6** *detail*
Arzak **31** *A6*
Astelena **10** *detail*
Bar Gorriti **9** *detail*
Bar Ondarra **1** *A6*
Bodegón Alejandro
  23 *detail*

Borda Berri **24** *detail*
Casa Gandarias **4** *detail*
Casa Urola **25** *detail*
Ganbara **7** *detail*
Garbola **8** *A6*
Goiz Argi **32** *detail*
Iturralde **33** *C5*
La Cuchara de
  San Telmo **12** *detail*
La Fábrica **34** *detail*
Ni Neu **17** *A5*
Petritegi **14** *C6*
Rekondo **35** *C1*
Txepetxa **36** *detail*
Zeruko **28** *detail*
Zuberoa **15** *C6*

Bars & clubs
Altxerri **15** *detail*
Bataplán **17** *C4*
Be Bop **29** *detail*
El Nido **19** *C5*
Museo del Whisky
  5 *detail*

ON THE ROAD
Bitter and twisted

You can't go far in the Basque lands without coming across a hauntingly contorted figure or sweep of rusted iron that signals a creation of Jorge de Oteiza or Eduardo Chillida. The powerful and original work of these two Basque sculptors is emblematic of the region.

Jorge de Oteiza, forthright and uncompromising well into his 90s, was born in Orio in 1908. After ditching a medical career in favour of sculpture he taught in South America. His big breakthrough came when commissioned to create pieces for the façade of the visionary new monastery at Arantzazu in the early 1950s. With his grey beard, leather jacket, beret and thick glasses, Oteiza cut quite a figure on site, but the anguish and power he managed to channel into his Apostles and Pietà was quite extraordinary. The Vatican prevented the erection of the 14 apostles for two decades. Oteiza was always preoccupied with relevance, famously saying that "a monument will be no more than a pile of stones or a coil of wire if it does not contribute to the making of a better human being, if it is not … the moulded key to a new kind of man". A museum in Navarra, in a house where he lived from 1975 onwards, holds a wide range of his work.

Eduardo Chillida was born in 1924 in San Sebastián and in his youth (and before a knee injury) appeared between the sticks for Real Sociedad. A sculptor of huge world renown, the spaces he created within his work are as important as the materials that comprise it. The Peine de los Vientos at San Sebastián and the Plaza de los Fueros in Vitoria are designed to interact dynamically with their setting, while his exploration of oxidized iron as a medium was particularly appropriate for Euskadi, built on the glories of a now-faded iron industry. Softer work in alabaster and wood is less confronting, but evokes the same theme of space. Chillida-Leku museum outside San Sebastián, currently closed, houses a large cross-section of his massive output.

The two sculptors were on bitter terms for many years: Oteiza, perhaps jealous of Chillida's rising profile, held the view that he had 'sold out', refused to use his name, and criticized him bitterly in public. Over the years there were accusations of plagiarism from both sides. Oteiza eventually had a change of heart and after many peaceful overtures were rejected, they finally buried the hatchet in 1997 with the 'Zabalaga embrace'. In fact, it seems that before Chillida's death in 2002, aged 78, they had become firm friends. Oteiza died only months later, in 2003, aged 94.

somewhat more spacious than La Concha and, at the end the town, gives way to the jagged rocky coastline of Guipúzcoa. Integrating the two is *El Peine del Viento*, the Comb of the Wind, one of sculptor Eduardo Chillida's (see box, above) signature works. It consists of three twisted rusty iron whirls, which, at times, seem to be struggling to tame the ragged breezes that can sweep the bay. After a vain attempt to borrow helicopters to place the sculptures, the task was finally accomplished using a specially designed floating bridge.

Monte Igueldo
€2.20 per person entrance by road or on foot.

Above Ondarreta rises the steep Monte Igueldo, which commands excellent views of all that is San Sebastián. It's not a place to meditate serenely over the panorama – the summit of the hill is capped by a luxury hotel and a slightly tacky **amusement park** ① *€2.20 per person*. The view makes it special though, and is unforgettable in the evening, when the city's lights spread out like a breaking wave below.

There's a **funicular** ① *1100-2000, roughly, check times on www.monteigueldo.es for exact operating hours, €1.75/3.15 return*, running from a station behind the tennis club at the end of the beach. Otherwise it's a walk up the winding road beside it, which gives occasional views both ways along the coast. To reach Ondarreta and the funicular, walk or take bus No 16 from Plaza Guipúzcoa.

Catedral del Buen Pastor
The simple and elegant neo-Gothic Catedral del Buen Pastor is light and airy with an array of geometric stained glass, but in reality, there's little to detain the visitor – it's more impressive outside than in. Lovers of kitsch art will, however, have a field day – the Christ with sheep above the altar is upstaged by the painted choirboy with donation box in hand.

Gros
low-key district appealing for its shops and surfer vibe

A bit more down-to-earth and relaxed than the rest of San Sebastián, Gros lies across the river and backs a good beach, which sees some decent surf. It's dominated by the Kursaal, but is also worth exploring for its off-the-beaten-track *pintxo* bars.

Kursaal
Av Zurriola 1, T943 003 000, www.kursaal.eus, guided tours Fri-Sun 1230, €3.

In a space that was derelict for three decades since the old Kursaal was demolished, these two stunning glass prisms opened their doors in 1999. Designed by Navarran architect Rafael Moneo to harmonize with the river mouth, the sea and 'communicate' with the hills of Uría and Urgull to either side, the concert hall has inspired much comment. The architect fondly refers to his building as 'two stranded rocks' – critics might agree – but the overall reaction has been very positive, and in 2001 the building won the European Union prize for contemporary architecture. The main building hosts concerts and conventions, while its smaller sidekick is an attractive exhibition centre. It's also the new home of the San Sebastián Film Festival and it houses a café and an upmarket modern restaurant as well. The Kursaal looks at its most impressive when reflecting the setting sun, or when lit up eerily at night.

Tabakalera
Plaza de las Cigarreras 1, T943 118 855, www.tabakalera.eu.

San Sebastián's enormous tobacco factory, behind the train station, has been regenerated as a cultural space and headquarters for several arts organizations. There are regular events, exhibitions and activities; check their website for what's on.

ON THE ROAD

The army of Christ

There can be few organizations that have had such an impact on all levels of world history than the Society of Jesus, or Jesuits. Their incident-filled five centuries of existence matches the strange life of their founder, Iñigo de Loiola, a Basque from a small town in the valleys of Guipúzcoa.

Born in 1491 to a wealthy family, Iñigo was the youngest of 13 children. Sent as a pageboy to the court of Castilla, he embarked on a life of gambling, womanizing and duelling. Fighting alongside his brother in an attempt to relieve the French siege of Pamplona, he was badly wounded in the legs by a cannonball. After being taken prisoner and operated on, he was sent home on a stretcher by the French, who admired his courage. His leg didn't mend, however, and it had to be rebroken and set. Although near to death several times, the bones eventually healed, but the vain Iñigo realized to his horror that a knob of bone still protruded from his leg, which had become shorter than the other. Desperate to strut his stuff as a dashing courtier again and despite anaesthetics not being available, he ordered the doctors to saw the bone off and lengthen the leg by repeated stretching.

During the boredom and pain of his lengthy convalescence, he began to read the only books at hand, the lives of the saints and a book on Jesus. Finally recovered in 1522, he set off on a journey, hoping to reach Jerusalem. Not far from home, riding muleback, he came across a Moor, with whom he argued about the virginity of Mary in her later life. When they parted company at a fork in the road, Iñigo decided that if

Around San Sebastián

green hills, cider culture and high gastronomy

Museo Chillida-Leku
Ctra Hernani–Rekalde, T943 336 006, www.museochillidaleku.com, closed at time of research.

The Museo Chillida-Leku is a very relaxing place to spend a few hours out of the city. The late Basque sculptor Eduardo Chillida (see box, page 66) gracefully restored a 16th-century farmhouse with his own concepts of angles and open interior space. The lower floor, lit by a huge window, has a selection of large pieces; upstairs is some of his smaller, earlier work, as well as preparatory drawings. Around the house is a large park, which has about 40 of his larger sculptures (these are changeable depending on exhibition commitments). It's a very peaceful and shady place to stroll; the organized should pack a picnic. At time of research it was closed indefinitely as the Basque government attempted to persuade the family to make it public again.

Cider houses
The tourist office in San Sebastián has a map and list of the cider houses, several are in very picturesque locations with walking trails through the hills and valleys from Astigarraga and Hernani, a 15-min bus ride from Plaza Guipúzcoa in the centre.

In the hills around Hernani and Astigarraga a short way south of town, apples are grown among stunning green hills. Although it's not hugely popular as a day-to-day drink in San

his mule followed the Moor, he would kill him, and if it went the other way, he would spare him. Luckily the mule went the other way.

After further enlightening experiences, and a spell in jail courtesy of the Inquisition, Iñigo ended up in Paris, meditating on what later became his Spiritual Exercises. His sceptical roommate was Francis Xavier, another Basque, whom Iñigo eventually won over. He and some companions travelled to Rome and, with the Pope's blessing, formed the Society of Jesus.

Iñigo died in 1556 and was canonized along with Francis Xavier in 1609. Since then the Jesuits, 41 saints on, have shared his passion for getting their hands dirty, being involved in education, charity and, more ominously, politics. They are a favoured target of conspiracy theorists, who have traditionally seen them as the real power behind the Vatican – the top Jesuit, the Superior General, is often called the 'Black Pope.'

For many centuries, however, the Jesuits were the prime educational force in western Europe and the New World: they have been called the 'schoolmasters of Europe'. The *reducciones*, communities of native Amerindians that they set up in Paraguay and Argentina were a brave and enlightened attempt to counteract slavery. These efforts, made famous by the film *The Mission*, were lauded by Voltaire (an unlikely source of praise) as "a triumph of humanity which seems to expiate the cruelties of the first conquerors". As a direct result of these works they were expelled from South America and Spain. In more recent times, the Jesuits have again courted the displeasure of western powers by advocating human rights in South America, so-called liberation theology seen as a grave danger to US muscle power in the region. The 2013 election of the Argentine Jesuit Jorge Mario Bergoglio to the papacy as Pope Francis is another intriguing chapter in the history of the order.

Sebastián these days, cider has an important place in Guipúzcoan history. It's nothing like your mass-produced commercial ciders, being sharpish, yeasty and not very fizzy. The cider is mostly made in the hills in the many small *sagardotegiak*, or *sidrerías*. When it's ready, in early January, cider houses stoke up their kitchens, dust down the tables and fling the doors open to the Donostian hordes, who spend whole afternoons eating massive traditional cider house meals and serving themselves freely from taps on the side of the vats. It's an excellent experience even if you're not sold on the cider itself. Tradition has it that this lasts until late April or so, although several are now open year-round.

The typical meal served starts with *tortilla de bacalao* (salt-cod omelette), continues with a massive slab of grilled ox, and concludes with cheese, walnuts, and *membrillo* (quince jelly, delicious with the cheese). The best of the places are the simpler rustic affairs with long, shared, rowdy wooden tables and floors awash with the apple brew, but these tend to be harder to get to. Expect to pay from €20-35 for the *menú sidrería*, which includes as much cider as you feel like sinking.

Tip...

Cider is best drunk fresh, poured from a height to give it some bounce after hitting the glass.

Guipúzcoa is criss-crossed by valleys that are lush from rainfall and dotted with small towns, agricultural centres for the surrounding farmland and some seats of heavier Basque industry such as cement or paper manufacture.

In many ways this is the 'real' Basqueland and the smaller, poorer communities are still where separatism flourishes most strongly. The valleys also conceal beautiful churches (as well as the massive Loiola basilica), and plenty of walks and picnic spots. Due to Euskadi's good transport connections, many of these places are within easy day-trip range of both San Sebastián and Bilbao. However, there are good accommodation options, especially in *casas rurales* or *agroturismos*, usually Basque farmhouses with good welcoming accommodation in the heart of the countryside.

Santuario de Loiola
Now here's a strange one. A massive **basilica** ⓘ *www.santuariodeloyola.org, daily 1000-1230, 1530-1815, €3, best time to visit is during the week as at weekends it's overcrowded with pilgrims*, not quite St Peter's or St Paul's but not very far off, standing in the middle of Guipúzcoan pasture land. All is explained by the fact that St Ignatius, founder of the Jesuits (see box, page 68) was born here. The house where he first saw daylight has bizarrely had the basilica complex built around it; it's now a museum.

The most arresting feature of the basilica from a distance is the massive dome, which stands 65 m high. Designed by Carlo Fontana, an Italian architect from Bernini's school, it's topped by an ornate cupola. Lavish is the word to describe the rest of the decoration of the church; minimalist gurus will probably drop dead on the spot. The building is designed to be viewed from a distance – this is the function of the formal promenade in front of it – and what first strikes the visitor are the harmonious proportions. On closer inspection, the intricacy of the decoration becomes apparent. Inside, the baroque style is grandiose (almost to the point of pomposity), with a silver-plated statue of Ignatius himself gazing serenely at some very elaborate stonework and massive slabs of marble.

Those with a keen interest in the saint might want to take themselves down to nearby **Azpeitia** to see the font where he was baptized, in the church of San Sebastián.

Oñati
The town of Oñati is one of the most attractive in the region and has a proud history as a university town and, until the mid-19th century, as a semi-independent fief of the local lord. The university, **Universidad de Sancti Spiritus**, was established in 1540 and is a beautiful example of cultured Renaissance architecture with an attractive colonnaded quadrangle. The stately red-balconied **Casa Consistorial** overlooks the main square where the two principal pedestrian streets, Calle Zaharra and Calle Barria, meet. These streets are the centre of the lively weekend nightlife as well as being the town's major axes.

Santuario de Arantzazu
Some 9 km south of Oñati is the Franciscan Santuario de Arantzazu, perching on a rock in a valley of great natural beauty. The basilica, built in the 1950s, is one of the most remarkable buildings in Euskadi. Incredibly avant-garde for the time, its spiky stone exterior is a reference to the hawthorn bush: according to tradition, a statue of Mary was found by a shepherd in 1468 on the spines of a hawthorn. A tinkling cowbell had led him to the spot, and the discovery ended years of war and famine in the area. The

statue now sits above the altar, surrounded by the visionary abstract altarpiece of Luzio Muñoz. Although it appears to be made of stone, it's actually treated wood, and 600 sq m of it at that. Above the iron doors, sculpted by Eduardo Chillida, are Jorge Oteiza's fluid apostles and *Pietà*. He created great controversy by sculpting 14 apostles; for years they lay idle near the basilica as the Vatican wouldn't permit them to be erected. In the crypt, the impressive paintings of Néstor Basterretxea also caused problems with the church hierarchy. He originally painted the crucifixion backwards; when this was censured, he agreed to repaint it but with an angry Jesus. He succeeded – his powerful red Christ is an imposing figure. See box, page 66, for further information on Oteiza and Chillida.

There are some excellent opportunities for walking in the area, which is one of the most beautiful parts of Euskadi.

Tolosa, Idiazábal and around

Lovers of quality farmland ingredients and untouristy villages should head east from Oñati (or south down the A1 from San Sebastián). The Goierri and Tolosaldea regions are ripe for exploration, with picturesque Basque countryside, traditional markets at Ordizia and Tolosa, home of Spain's most famous *alubia* (bean) and the village that gives its name to and is the centre of production for one of Spain's finest cheeses, Idiazábal. The **Parque Natural Aralar** flanks the Navarran border and offers some good walking. An adventure park at its entrance, www.txindokikoitzala.com, offers good activities for all ages.

Listings San Sebastián/Donostia *map page 64.*

Tourist information

Oñati tourist office
Plaza de los Fueros.

San Sebastián tourist office
Boulevard 8, T943 481 166,
www.sansebastianturismo.com.
Mid-Jun to mid-Sep Mon-Sat 0900-2000,
Sun 1000-1900, mid-Sep to mid-Jun
Mon-Sat 0900-1900, Sun 1000-1400.
The efficient, English-speaking office is busy but helpful. You can download city information to your mobile phone here. There's also a summer information kiosk on the beach promenade. The tourist office runs a booking agency for accommodation and events, T902 443 442, www.sansebastianreservas.com.

Where to stay

The Parte Vieja is the best spot for budget accommodation, with an unbelievable number of *pensiones*, some quite luxurious; there's also some near the cathedral

around C San Martín. All accommodation in San Sebastián is overpriced; there is no getting away from the fact. High season is Jun-Sep; prices are at least 30% lower in most places outside this period. Be aware that the pedestrianized part of the old town can be extremely noisy at night, especially at weekends.

€€€€ Hotel de Londres y de Inglaterra
C Zubieta 2, T943 440 770, www.hlondres.com.
Grand old beachfront hotel that is an emblem of the city's glory days. It wears its age comfortably, and refitted rooms offer plenty of comfort. If royalty don't drop by as often as they once did, no one's letting on. Spend the extra for a room with the stunning bay view.

€€€€ Hotel María Cristina
C República Argentina 4, T943 437 600,
www.hotel-mariacristina.com.
Taking up an entire block, its elegant sandstone bulk has cradled more celebrities than you could drop a fork at. A refit has left it looking stunning, and it's a 5-star experience in every way. It has all the

services, luxury, and style you would expect, including a child-minding service and a proper concierge, as well as prices that boot other Basque hotels into the campsite class. The rooms are huge, with ultra-comfortable beds, and blend an appropriate classicism with modern swirls of colour.

€€€€ Villa Soro
Av de Ategorrieta 61, T943 297 970, www.villasoro.es.
To the east of Gros, this sumptuous 19th-century villa is something of an oasis, set in large grounds with manicured gardens. It really feels like a rural hotel, with discreet service, a refined, relaxing feel, and seriously comfortable rooms, some in an annexe. No restaurant (but wonderful Arzak is a short walk away). Free bikes offer a good way to zip around town. Recommended.

€€€ Pensión Gran Bahía Bernardo
C Embeltrán 16, T943 420 216, www. pensiongranbahiabernardo.com.
This attractive and upmarket *pensión* is convenient for both the beach and Parte Vieja. The beds are very comfortable, and the rooms well equipped, a/c and quietish. There are a few different room categories. €€ off-season.

€€ Izar Bat
C Fermín Calbetón 6, T943 431 573, www.pensionizarbat.com.
Kitted out in warm colours and with bathrooms so bright and clean you need sunglasses, this is a top Parte Vieja budget option. High beds are extremely comfortable, there are modern facilities and a fridge in every room, and the front rooms are double glazed to avoid the worst of the noise.

€€ Pensión Aída
C Iztueta 9, Gros, T943 327 800, www.pensionesconencanto.com.
A very good place to stay in Gros, and convenient for the station. The gleaming rooms are appealing, and the breakfast in bed is a great way to start the day. There's free Wi-Fi and internet, and they rent bikes. Recommended.

€€ Pensión Altair
C Padre Larroca 3, T943 293 133, www.pension-altair.com.
Gleaming, friendly, and with a decent location in Gros, this stylish and comfortable choice takes the humble *pensión* to stratospheric levels. With modern conveniences like free Wi-Fi, swipe cards and safes in the rooms, decorated with a soft contemporary scheme, this is one of the city's best. Book it ahead. Recommended.

€€ Pensión Amaiur
C 31 de Agosto 44, T943 429 654, www.pensionamaiur.com.
Situated in the oldest house in the Parte Vieja (few others survived the 1813 fire), this is one of the best budget options in town. Lovingly decorated and sympathetically run, there's a variety of smallish but homely rooms (some sharing a bathroom between 2), most with satellite TV and some with balconies. Guests have free use of the pretty (stoveless) kitchen. Recommended.

€€ Pensión Kursaal
C Peña y Goñi 2, T943 292 666, www.pensionkursaal.com.
A good place to stay just across the river in Gros, and very near the beach. The attractive rooms have large windows, bathrooms and TV. As in many of these old buildings, the plumbing and heating can make a racket. Parking available under the Kursaal for a good price.

€€ Pensión San Lorenzo
C San Lorenzo 2, T943 425 516, www.pensionsanlorenzo.com.
A friendly star of the old town near the Bretxa market. The 5 well-priced rooms are brightly decorated and come with full facilities including fridge. It's a quiet place and not luxurious but offers good value for this pricey town.

€€ Pensión San Martín
C San Martín 10, T943 428 714, www.pensionsanmartin.com.

One of the better of the host of choices on this street. The rooms are good and comfy, and have bathrooms and TV. Very handy for the train and bus stations.

Camping

Camping Igueldo
Paseo Padre Orkolaga 69, T943 214 502, www.campingigueldo.net. Open all year.
This big San Sebastián campsite is back from Ondarreta beach behind Monte Igueldo. They've got bungalows, and it's easily accessed on bus No 16 from near the tourist office.

Santuario de Loiola

€€ Hotel Loiola
Av de Loiola s/n, Loiola, T943 151 616, www.hotelloiola.com.
Although the building itself won't win many prizes for harmonious rural architecture, it's handy for the basilica, and reasonable value. The rooms are a touch dull but don't lack conveniences.

Oñati
The cheaper beds in Oñati fill up quickly at weekends.

€€ Ongi Etorri
C Zaharra 19, T943 718 285, www.hotelongi.com.
This family-run hotel is well located on the main pedestrian street. The rooms are thoughtfully decorated, a touch small, but snug with heating and a/c.

€€ Torre de Zumeltzegi
C Torre Zumeltzegi 11, T943 540 000, www.hoteltorrezumeltzegi.com.
This fabulously restored medieval tower offers the best place to stay for some distance. Utterly characterful, the interior (and modern annexe) offers comfort and an excellent welcome. It's surrounded by fields but only a few mins' stroll from the centre, which it overlooks from its perch atop a hill. There's a decent restaurant too. Recommended.

€ Arregi
Ctra Garagaltza-Auzoa 21, T943 780 824, www.casaruralarregi.es.
An excellent *agroturismo* a couple of kilometres from Oñati. A big farmhouse in a green valley with beautiful dark-wood rooms, a ping-pong table, and pleasant owners. You can use the kitchen, or they can provide dinner with advance notice. Recommended.

Santuario de Arantzazu
There are a couple of hotels and restaurants in Arantzazu but, happily, nothing else.

€€ Hotel Santuario de Arantzazu
Arantzazu 29, T943 781 313, www.hotelsantuariodearantzazu.com.
Right next to the basilica, this monk-run guesthouse has been converted to a modern hotel with spa and conference facilities. It's all very comfortable, but the restaurant leaves a bit to be desired. Great location.

Restaurants

San Sebastián is the gourmet capital of Spain, with some seriously classy restaurants dotting the city and the hills around. Several of the nation's finest eateries are here; as well as those we list, **Akelarre** (www.akelarre.net), **Martín Berasategui** (www.martinberasategui.com) and **Mugaritz** (www.mugaritz.com) are gourmet temples in and around town. It's also a great place for crawling around bars eating *pintxos*; the best zone for this is the Parte Vieja, where 'eat street' is C Fermín Calbetón, with several excellent places. Gros is a quieter but equally tasty option. Cold *pintxos* are arranged on the bartops here, but most places offer hot ones cooked to order. These can be a real highlight – look out for the board listing them. To order, get a waiters attention and say, for example, 'dos de foie' (2 foie *pintxos*). Pintxos cost €2.50-4. Eating in the city is far from cheap by Spanish standards. If you're here in spring, make sure you make a trip into the hills to one of the many cider houses (*sagardotegiak*) around the towns of Hernani and Astigarraga for no-frills good cheer, eating, and drinking. See www.sagardotegiak.com for a list of these establishments.

€€€ Arzak
Av Alcalde José Elósegui 243, T943 278 465, www.arzak.info.
On a hill in the eastern reaches of town, this is many foodies' choice as Spain's top restaurant and it doesn't disappoint. The Arzak family has been running it for over a century, and it maintains some of that traditional atmosphere; it's no aloof gastronomic Parnassus, though the interior is darkly contemporary. The quality and innovation doesn't come cheap though. The degustation menu (€226 plus drinks) is the way to go here. Highly recommended.

€€€ Bodegón Alejandro
C Fermín Calbetón 4, T943 427 158, www.bodegonalejandro.com.
This popular spot has a homely, unpretentious interior; the focus is on the quality cuisine, which draws influences both from the new Basque wave and from upmarket French bistro traditions. Eating is via a bistro menu and might see you follow crab ravioli with roast trotters. Drinks are extra.

€€€ Rekondo
Paseo de Igueldo 57, T943 212 907, www.rekondo.com.
On the slopes of the Igueldo hill, with great views, this offers traditional but upmarket Basque cuisine that includes excellent grilled meats and well-treated fish. The real highlight is the wine cellar. With some 100,000 bottles, this is one of the nation's top wine collections.

€€€ Zuberoa
Barrio Iturriotz 8, T943 491 228, www.zuberoa.com.
Outside San Sebastián, near the town of Oiartzun/Oyarzun is the lair of top chef Hilario Arbelaitz, in an attractive stone farmhouse with a wooden porch and terrace. Arbelaitz combines an essential Basqueness with a treatment inspired by the very best of French and Mediterranean cuisine. Everything is delicious, from a typical fish soup to the untypical grapefruit, spider crab and trout roe jelly with potato and olive oil cream. The degustation menu focuses on flavour more than fanciness and is a memorable feast.

€€ A Fuego Negro
C 31 de Agosto, T650 135 373, www.afuegonegro.com.
Darkly modish and moody in red and black, this bar has become one of Donostia's in-vogue eating options. A bewildering mixture of Euskara and Spanish covers the blackboard – ask the waiter to recommend something or for the English translation if you're not sure what they're on about. The *pintxo* combinations are incredibly imaginative; they don't all work but you can have fun trying. Pricier than most *pintxo* bars.

€€ Astelena
C Euskal Herría 3, T943 425 867, www.restauranteastelena.com.
In a quiet side street near the Bretxa market, this modern place buzzes with chat during the week, when its *menú* (available lunch Tue-Fri and dinner Tue-Thu), using fresh market produce, pulls in the punters. It offers excellent value for its stylish cuisine at any time.

€€ Casa Urola
C Fermín Calbetón 20, T943 441 371, www.casaurolajatetxea.es.
An enticing choice whether for *pintxos* or a full meal, this small and busy bar has exquisite gourmet snacks on the counter. There are 2 dining areas; upstairs is more

> **Tip...**
> Several of Spain's finest restaurants are in and around San Sebastián, so make sure to book those special degustation dinners as far ahead as possible.

Gastroclubs

An unusual aspect of the eating culture in the Basque Country are the *txokos*, or gastronomic societies, whose spiritual home is San Sebastián. These are private clubs whose three key parts are a members' lounge, a dining room and a vast kitchen. The members gather to swap recipes and prepare massive gourmet meals to be devoured by themselves, friends, and family.

Traditionally, *txokos* were all male societies, but in recent years most have opened the doors to women too, though it's common for the kitchen to still be a men-only preserve. As these *txokos* are invitation-only, you're unlikely to be able to experience one unless you know a member, although **San Sebastián Food** (see What to do, page 78) offer the chance to visit one.

peaceful. The fish dishes are excellent and the *solomillo*'s tasty too. Recommended.

€€ Ganbara
C San Jerónimo 21, T943 422 575,
www.ganbarajatetxea.com.
This is a fairly upmarket tapas bar and *asador* with a worthwhile array of *pintxos* to accompany the cheerfully poured wine. The *raciones* are delicious, with such delicacies as *trufas* (truffles) and *percebes* (goose barnacles) making an appearance.

€€ La Fábrica
C Puerto 17, T943 432 110,
www.restaurantelafabrica.es.
If *pintxo*-hopping is all getting a bit much and you want a sit-down meal without sacrificing quality or maxing out the credit card, head here. A good-quality set menu is only €31 lunch or dinner during the week (€41 at weekends), and is accompanied by friendly service in this stylishly appointed but comfortable space.

€€ Petritegi
Camino de Petritegi 6, Astigarraga,
T943 457 188, www.petritegi.com.
Dinner only, and lunch at weekends.
In the cidery hills near town, this is one of the few *sagardotegiak* (cider houses) to open year-round. The traditional cod omelette is excellent, and you pour your own cider straight from the barrel. Set menus are €28-36.

€ Bar Gorriti
C San Juan 3, T943 428 353,
www.bargorriti.com.
An unglamorous bar that's been going since the 1920s. Somewhat surprisingly, on entering you are confronted with a mighty impressive spread of cold *pintxos* during the day and early evening. You could spend all day in here if you weren't careful. A great spot and an antidote to the overelaboration in some of the newer places.

€ Bar Ondarra
Av de la Zurriola 16, T943 326 033.
Opposite the Kursaal exhibition centre in Gros, this is a no-frills tapas bar with a small street level and an underground den featuring regular live jazz and soul. Good cold *pintxos*.

€ Borda Berri
C Fermín Calbetón 12, T943 430 342.
The checked tiles and *pintxo*-free wooden bar make it feel like you've stepped into another country suddenly. But once you get your lips around the melt-in-the-mouth foie, the slow-cooked duck magret, or the *carrillera* (cheek), you're back in gourmet heaven. All prepared to order. Recommended.

€ Casa Gandarias
C 31 de Agosto 25, T943 426 362,
www.restaurantegandarias.com.
This busy tapas bar is near the Santa María church and has an adjoining restaurant.

The *pintxos* are excellent and are served by efficient and cordial staff. The *solomillo* or the grilled foie are particularly recommended. Good whisky selection, too.

€ Garbola
Paseo Colón 11, T943 285 019.
Legendary for its scrumptious mushroom creations and *caipirinhas*, this Gros bar also offers more unusual snacks, such as kangaroo and shark. It's very plush and old-fashioned inside.

€ Goiz Argi
C Fermín Calbetón 4, T943 425 204.
A warmly welcoming family-run place, this specializes in skewered *pintxos*. The hot ones are very tasty: prawns with a spicy garlic and chilli sauce might have you ordering seconds.

€ La Cuchara de San Telmo
C 31 de Agosto 28 (back), T943 435 446,
www.lacucharadesantelmo.com.
An extraordinary bar up the side of the museum. The Cuchara's tiny open kitchen pioneered the idea of *pintxos* in the form of made-to-order gourmet dishes in miniature, now something found in several of Donostia's bars. There's a short, changing menu, but everything is delicious. It's an inspiring and down-to-earth place. Recommended.

€ Txepetxa
C Pescadería 5, T943 422 227,
www.bartxepetxa.com.
Nobody seems to like anchovies any more, but you'll like these: the fresh kind, not the salted ones. They come in myriad ways, advertised by lifelike plastic models. With foie gras and apple? Doesn't sound like it'd work, but it does.

€ Zeruko
C Pescadería 10, T943 423 451,
www.barzeruko.com.
Don't mind the sawdust on the floor, this is a very smart bar that produces *pintxos* and *raciones* of the highest class. The main dishes are based around stew-type meals, with *chipirones en su tinta* (squid in ink) particularly

delicious. The bar snacks are so elaborate you'll have to ask what most of them are.

Cafés

Iturralde
Av Libertad 11, T943 428 690,
www.cafeiturralde.com.
You might struggle to squeeze into this narrow spot, but it's worth it. There's really excellent coffee and teas and infusions bursting with flavour. The owner knows what she's doing, so if she suggests something say yes. Recommended.

Ni Neu
Av Zurriola 1, T943 003 162,
www.restauranteninneu.com.
The outdoor part of this Kursaal restaurant is an excellent spot for an early evening *pintxo* and drink, with superb views over the river mouth and sea.

Oñati
The **Zelai-Zabal** (www.zelaizabal.com) in Arantzazu has a sound reputation as serving the area's best food.

Bars and clubs

The Parte Vieja has many options and the crossroads of C Larramendi and C Reyes Católicos near the cathedral is full of bars. There's studeny nightlife around C San Bartolomé, just back from the beach.

Altxerri Bar
C Reina Regenta 2. Open 1700 to late.
An atmospheric cellar bar by the tourist office that regularly showcases live jazz and other acts. Draws an interesting crowd and is worthwhile even if there's nothing on.

Bataplán
Playa de la Concha 10, T943 473 601,
www.bataplandisco.com.
San Sebastián's most famous *discoteca*, right on La Concha beach. Thu-Sat from 2400 and attracts a smart young crowd. The music is mostly club anthems and pop crowd

pleasers. Rises to prominence during the film festival when it hosts various after-parties. The upstairs bar is a nice place for a drink overlooking the beach. €7-15 entry.

Be Bop
Paseo de Salamanca 3, T943 429 869, www.barbebop.com.
This well-visited bar by the river mouth is quiet and relaxing and has regular live jazz music playing; at time of research it was closed for major renovation but due to reopen.

El Nido
C Larramendi 13, T943 473 322.
A sizeable pub that fills after work and doesn't empty again until late. Friendly crowd and board games.

Museo del Whisky
Alameda Boulevard 5, T943 424 678, www.museodelwhisky.com.
Elegant and refined, this 2-level bar does indeed have a sizeable whisky collection on shelves all around. The mixed drinks are pricy and delicious, and there's an atmosphere of well-heeled good cheer.

Entertainment

Football club
Estadio de Anoeta, *Paseo de Anoeta 1, T943 462 833, www.realsociedad.com.* This is the home of **Real Sociedad**, the city's football team. Given the title 'Real' (Royal) in 1910 by the king, who spent much time in the city, the club is one of comparatively few to have won the Spanish league title. Tickets €25-50 (sold at the stadium from the Thu afternoon before a game to the Sat evening, then 2 hrs before kick-off.

Theatre
The beautiful **Teatro Victoria Eugenia** is a sparklingly atmospheric place to catch a show, and benefits greatly from its recent restoration. The box office, T943 481 818, www.victoriaeugenia.com, is open 1130-1330, 1700-2000; there's also a good café-restaurant.

Festivals

19-20 Jan Tamborrada, the feast day of San Sebastián, is celebrated with a deafening parade of drummers through the streets from midnight on the 19th.
2nd fortnight of Jul International Jazz Festival (www.heinekenjazzaldia.com).
1st fortnight of Aug Classical Fortnight (www.quincenamusical.com). Spain's oldest classical music festival.
Week before 15 Aug Aste Nagusia or 'big week', the city's major fiesta, kicks off in San Sebastián with world-renowned fireworks exhibitions.
3rd week of Sep International Film Festival (www.sansebastianfestival.com).

Shopping

La Bretxa, *Plaza de Bretxa, Market complex in the Old Town.* The food market downstairs is the best bit.
Solbes, *C Aldamar 4, T943 427 818.* A delicatessen and wine shop with a high-quality, not particularly cheap line-up.
Zaporejai, *C San Jerónimo 21, T943 422 882, www.zaporejai.com.* In the old town, this place sells a variety of excellent hams. It's a friendly spot, and they'll be pleased to explain about piggy products and let you taste things.

What to do

Boat trips
The boat *Ciudad San Sebastián*, T670 201 155, www.ciudadsansebastian.com, runs ½-hr trips around the bay, with hourly departures daily in summer and at weekends in spring and autumn, €10 (leaves from halfway along aquarium wharf).

City tours
The tourist office offers recommended guided walking tours (€10). There's a hop-on, hop-off bus that runs Fri-Sun from mid-Nov to mid-Mar, and daily mid-Mar to mid-Nov. Ticket (€12) valid for 24 hrs.

There's also a small tourist train (www.sansebastianturismo.com) running around the streets. It leaves every hour from Paseo Salamanca next to the river (€5).

Food tours

San Sebastián Food, *T943 421 143, www.sansebastianfood.com*. An excellent English-speaking set-up that offers various gourmet options from *pintxo* tours of the old town – a good way to get the hang of this sometimes intimidating way of eating – *pintxo* cookery classes, wine tastings, Rioja visits and more. You can book online.

Language schools

Lacunza, C Mundaiz 8, T943 326 680, www.lacunza. com; **Tandem San Sebastián**, C Pasajes 4, T943 326 705, www.tandemsansebastian.com.

Transport

Bicycle hire

Bici Rent Donosti, Av de la Zurriola 22, T943 271 173, www.bicirentdonosti.es. Open daily 0900-2100, this shop on Gros beach rents bikes by the hour and by the day. They're not cheap at €18 per day, but there's a decent range, and the staff will help with planning trips.

Bus

The main bus station, www.estaciondonostia.com, is a flash new affair opposite the train station, with lots of platforms and luggage lockers.

Bilbao (1 hr 10 mins) is served at least hourly, and **Vitoria** (1 hr 40 mins) 7 or more times a day.

Other destinations include **Pamplona** (8 daily, 1 hr 15 mins), **Madrid** (11 daily, 5 hrs 45 mins), **Burgos** (4 daily, 3-4 hrs), and **Santander** (9 daily, 3-4 hrs). There are also buses to **Bayonne** and **Biarritz** in France.

Shorter-haul buses to Guipúzcoan destinations leave from the central Plaza Guipúzcoa and the streets around this area. Destinations include **Zumaia**, **Zarautz**, **Azkoitia** and **Loiola** (the exception; this leaves from the bus station), **Tolosa**, **Oiartzun**, **Hernani**, **Astigarraga**, all with very frequent departures.

Train

There are mainline train departures to **Madrid** (6 daily, 5 hrs 30 mins to 7 hrs 30 mins) and other Spanish cities.

There are 7 trains a day for **Vitoria** (1 hr 40 mins). **Euskotren** connects the city with other Basque destinations on the coast and inland: its hub is Amara, on Plaza Easo in the south part of the new town. **Bilbao** is served hourly via the coast (2 hrs 40 mins). **El Topo** (the Mole) is a train service running from Amara to **Hendaye** in France, it runs every 10-15 mins and takes 35 mins. At Hendaye you can change to mainline **SNCF** train services.

Santuario de Loiola
Bus

You can reach Azkoitia and Loiola by bus from **Bilbao's** bus station (3 a day), and from **San Sebastián** (hourly, 1 hr) (destination may be marked 'Azpeitia').

Oñati
Bus

Oñati is accessed by bus from **Bilbao's** bus station with **Pesa** once daily Mon-Fri, otherwise connect with local bus from **Bergara**. There's no public transport from Oñati to **Arantzazu** except a Sun bus service; a taxi costs about €12 each way. Walking from Oñati takes about 2 hrs, but the return trip downhill is significantly quicker. There's plenty of traffic, and it's easy to hitch a ride.

Guipúzcoan
Coast

Crossing the French border, the first stretches of Spain are well worth investigating, starting with the very first town. Hondarribia is a beautiful walled place completely free of the malaise that seems to afflict most border towns; if you don't mind a few day trippers, this is one of the most attractive towns in Euskadi. It's a good place to stay, but is easily reached as an excursion from San Sebastián too.

The coast west of San Sebastián is characterized by some fairly muscular cliffs interspersed with a few excellent beaches, a popular summer playground. As with Vizcaya, the area's history is solidly based on the fishing of anything and everything from anchovies to whales. While Zarautz's aim in life seems to be to try and emulate on a smaller scale its big brother San Sebastián just along the coast, Getaria is a particularly attractive little port.

Hondarribia/Fuenterrabia

This old fishing port sits at the mouth of the Río Bidasoa looking directly across at France, a good deal more amicably now than for much of its history. The well-preserved 15th-century walls weren't erected just for decoration, and the city has been besieged more times than it cares to remember.

Although there's a fishing port, very busy marina, and a decent beach, the most charming area of Hondarribia is the walled part, a hilly grid of cobbled streets entered through arched gates. The stone used for many of the venerable old buildings seems to be almost luminous in the evening sun. The hill is topped by a plaza and a 16th-century **Palace of Carlos V**, now a parador; its imposing bulk is offset by a very pretty courtyard. Nearby, the **Iglesia de Santa María de Manzano** is topped by a belltower and an impressive coat-of-arms. It was here in 1660 that María Teresa, daughter of Felipe IV, married Louis XIV of France, the Sun King. **Plaza Guipúzcoa** is even nicer than the main square, with cobbles and small but ornate buildings overhanging a wooden colonnade.

Outside the walls, the marina is busy with yachts and sits at the river mouth, just behind the beach. It's worth exploring the headland beyond here. Passing the fishing harbour, you reach a lighthouse with spectacular views. Below here, the Asturiaga bay has some remains from its days as a Roman anchorage. Above it is a small fort, the Castillo de San Telmo, not open to the public.

Hondarribia makes an excellent place to stay, with several appealing hotels and top restaurants.

Irún

Near Hondarribia, the town of Irún is joined by road and rail to Hendaye in France but has little of interest except **Museo Oiasso** ① *Eskoleta 1, T943 639 353, www.oiasso.com, Sep-Mar Tue-Thu and Sun 1000-1400, Fri-Sat 1000-1400, 1600-1900, Apr-Aug Tue-Sat 1000-2000, Sun 1000-1400, €6,* attractively displaying finds from the ancient Roman settlement here of the same name. South of town, there's good walking on the hills of the Aiako Harria natural park.

Pasaia/Pasajes

West of Hondarribia, the GI-3440 rises steeply, affording some fantastic views over a long stretch of coastline. Between Hondarribia and San Sebastián, it's worth stopping at Pasaia/Pasajes, the name given to a group of towns clustering around a superb natural harbour 6 km east of San Sebastián. **Pasai Donibane** (Pasajes San Juan), distinct from the other parts that are devoted to large-scale shipbuilding, is a very charming town that literally only has one street, which wends its way along the water, twisting around some buildings and simply going through others. While now dwarfed by the industry across the water, this was for periods in history the most important Basque port. The Romans made use of it to export mining products; whaling expeditions boldly set off for some very far-flung destinations indeed; and a good part of the Spanish Armada was built and crewed from this area. A later boost was given to the town as a result of the chocolate trade with Venezuela but by the time Victor Hugo came to live here for a spell, it was no longer the shipping centre it had been. His house now holds the tourist office and an exhibition on his life. See below for opening hours.

Pasaia gets a fair number of French tourists strolling through, which means that there are several restaurants (although, at time of writing, no accommodation apart from a hostel for pilgrims and a rural guesthouse outside town). Apart from eating and strolling, you might want to investigate **Albaola** ⓘ *T943 392 426, www.albaola.com, Tue-Sun 1000-1400, 1500-1900 (1800 Oct-Easter), €7*, an organization that builds traditional Basque boats, such as were used in Pasaia's heyday. Currently they are working on a whaling boat, the *San Juan*. It's in nearby Pasai San Pedro; see the website for info on how to get there.

Listings East of San Sebastián

Tourist information

Hondarribia

Tourist office
Arma Plaza 9, T943 643 677, www. bidasoaturismo.com. Jul to mid-Sep daily 0930-1930, mid-Sep to Jun 1000-1800.
The town's main tourist office. There's another office at the marina.

Pasaia

Tourist office
In Victor Hugo's old house, www.oarsoaldea turismoa.eus. Sep-Jun Mon-Sat 1000-1400 and 1600-1800, Sun 1000-1400, Jul-Aug daily 0900-1400 and 1600-1900.
Their website gives ideas for activities in the area.

Where to stay

Hondarribia

€€€€ Parador de Hondarribia
Plaza de Armas 14, T943 645 500, www.parador.es.
This fortress was originally constructed in the 10th century, then reinforced by Carlos V to resist French attacks. Behind the beautiful façade is a hotel of considerable comfort and delicacy, although the rooms don't reach the ornate standard set by the public areas. A pretty courtyard and terrace are the highlights.

€€€ Hotel Jaizkibel
Baserritar Etorbidea 1, T943 646 040, www.hoteljaizkibel.com.
Named for the mountain that separates Hondarribia from San Sebastián, this modern

hotel hits plenty of heights of its own. Spacious, frippery-free rooms and a tranquil but central location makes this ideal for relaxation, and the views and solicitous staff seal the deal.

€€€ Hotel Obispo
Plaza del Obispo s/n, T943 645 400, www.hotelobispo.com.
The former archbishop's palace is also over-flowing with character; it's a beautiful building and features some pleasant views across the Bidasoa. The rooms are delightful, particularly on the top floor. Free internet access and frequent special offers. Recommended.

€€ Hotel Palacete
Plaza Guipúzcoa 5, T943 640 813, www.hotelpalacete.net.
Winningly situated on Hondarribia's prettiest plaza, and with modern, compact rooms with a colourful, airy feel, this hotel offers good value and welcoming service in the heart of things. There's a pleasing garden patio for quiet moments.

€€ Pensión Txoko-Goxoa
C Murrua 22, T943 644 658, www.txokogoxoa.com.
A pretty little place in a peaceful part of town by the town walls (enter from the street below). Rooms small but homely, with flowers in the window boxes, and spotlessly clean. It's overpriced for a simple *pensión*, but the location is good.

Camping

Faro de Higuer
Paseo del Faro 58, T943 641 008, www.campingfarodehiguer.es.

One of 2 decent campsites, slightly closer to town on the way to the lighthouse. Great location. There's a pool, lively bar, and a few bungalows.

Restaurants

Hondarribia
The town is notable for its excellent restaurants; the location between San Sebastián and France is propitious.

€€€ Alameda
C Minasoroeta 1, T943 642 789, www.restaurantealameda.net.
Pushing hard for the Hondarribia gold medal, this exquisite spot serves elaborate gourmet dishes with a confident, well-presented flair. The short menu is bolstered by appealing daily specials, and there are also 3 multi-course set menus to choose from.

€€€ Sebastián
C Mayor 9, T943 640 167, www.sebastian hondarribia.com. Closed Nov and Mon.
This excellent restaurant is attractively set in a dingy old grocery packed with interesting aromas. The food goes far beyond the humble decor, with a good-value *menú de degustación*.

€€ Arroka Berri
Higer Bidea 6, T943 642 712, www.arrokaberri.com.
With a lovely setting near the lighthouse, this is an Hondarribia classic. Top-quality produce prepared in succulent ways with an eye on presentation and innovation but no faff. Family-friendly.

€ Ardoka
C San Pedro 32, T943 643 169, www.ardokavinoteka.com.
A spectacular *pintxo* option on this fertile new town street, with an intriguing selection of wines to match.

€ Gran Sol
C San Pedro 62, T943 647 075, www.bargransol.com.
Absolutely top-quality *pintxos* in this bar, which have won a variety of awards. The attached restaurant is run by the chef's partner and is also excellent.

Transport

Hondarribia
Boat
Boats run across the river to the French town of **Hendaye**.

Bus
There are buses to and from Plaza Guipúzcoa in **San Sebastián** every 20 mins. A few buses cross the border into France. There are frequent buses linking Hondarribia with **Irún**, just a few kilometres down the road, from where there's more regular cross-border transport to neighbouring **Hendaye**.

Train
The most common way of crossing the border is by the *topo* train that burrows through the mountain from between **San Sebastián** or **Irún** and **Hendaye**. Irún is an easy cab ride from Hondarribia.

Pasaia
Bus
Buses run every 20 mins to Pasaia from Plaza Guipúzcoa in **San Sebastián**.

picturesque fishing ports and sandy beaches

Orio

This little fishing port sits on the Oria River not far from the sea. It's famous for *besugo* (sea bream) and has plenty of character in the climbing medieval lanes of its old town. It's also well known for having the rowing club that's traditionally the strongest in the *trainera* regattas in these parts. Yellow flags hung from balconies express support for the local team.

Zarautz

While similarly blessed with a beautiful stretch of sandy beach and a characterful old town, like its neighbour San Sebastián, Zarautz, a couple of kilometres west of Orio, has suffered from quick-buck beachfront high-rise development, which seems to appeal to the moneyed set who descend here by the thousand during the summer months. Nevertheless, along with the rows of bronzed bodies and the prudish but colourful changing tents, it can be a fun place. There's a good long break for surfing – one of the rounds of the world championship is often held here – and there's scope for more unusual watersports too.

The old town is separated from the beach by the main road, giving Zarautz a slightly disjointed feel. There are a few well-preserved medieval structures, such as the **Torre Luzea**, and a handful of decent bars. Zarautz is known for its classy restaurants; after all, there's more to a Basque beach holiday than fish 'n' chips.

★ Getaria/Guetaria

Improbably perched on a hunk of angled slate, Getaria is well worth a stop en route between Bilbao and San Sebastián. Despite being a large-scale fish cannery, the town is picturesque with cobbled streets winding their way to the harbour and, bizarrely, through an arch in the side of the church.

Getaria gets its fair share of passing tourists, which is reflected in the number of *asadores* that line its harbour and old centre. For an unbeatable authentic local feed, order a bottle of sprightly local *txakolí* and wash it down with a plate of grilled sardines – you'll turn your nose up at the canned variety for ever more.

The **Iglesia de San Salvador** is intriguing, even without the road that passes under it. The wooden floor lists at an alarming angle; to the faithful in the pews the priest seems to be saying Mass from on high.

You won't stay long without coming across a statue of **Juan Sebastián Elkano**, winner of Getaria's most famous citizen award for nearly 500 years running, although fashion designer Cristóbal Balenciaga has come close in more recent times. Elkano, who set sail in 1519 on an expedition captained by Magellan, took command after the skipper was murdered in the Philippines. Sailing into Sevilla with the scant remnants of the expedition's crew, he thus became the first to circumnavigate the world. Not a bad finish for someone who had mutinied against the captain only a few months after leaving port.

Beyond the harbour, the wooded hump of San Antón is better known as **El Ratón** (the mouse), for its resemblance to that rodent. There are good views from the highest point – pass by the lighthouse at its tip and continue upwards; if the weather is clear you can see the coast of France northwards on the horizon.

Behind Getaria, a country road winds its way into the hills through the vineyards of the local *txakolí* producers. It makes a pleasant stroll from town, rewarded with some spectacular coastal views.

Zumaia/Zumaya

Some 5 km further along, Zumaia is not quite as attractive, but is another pleasant seaside and fishing town and has the worthwhile **Museo Zuloaga** ⓘ *Ctra San Sebastián–Bilbao, T677 078 445, www.espaciozuloaga.com, mid-Jun to Aug Fri-Sat 1600-2000, Sep Sat 1600-2000, €10.* Ignacio Zuloaga, born in 1870, was a prominent Basque painter and a member of the so-called 'Generation of 98', a group of artists and thinkers who symbolized Spain's intellectual revival in the wake of the loss of the Spanish-American War, known as 'the disaster'. Zuloaga lived in this pretty house and garden, which now contains some of his works as well as other paintings he owned, including some Spanish Masters. Zuloaga himself is most admired for his expressive portraiture, with subjects frequently depicted against a typically bleak Spanish landscape. In the best of his work, the faces of the painted have a deep wisdom and a deep sadness that seems to convey both the artist's love and hatred for his country. Opening times are limited, but the enthusiastic guided tour gives you a good feel for the artist's life. The museum is a 15-minute walk on the Getaria/San Sebastián road from the centre of Zumaia.

The stretch of coastline west of Zumaia has an 8-km-long stretch of spectacular cliffs. It's part of the **Basque Coast Geopark** ⓘ *www.geoparkea.com*, notable for its inland karstic formations and here, along the shore, its weird flysch formations. There's a coastal footpath from Zumaia to Deba and beyond to Mutriku, but guided visits from Zumaia, with both foot and boat segments, are the best way to understand the geology. Some guides speak English – contact tourist offices in any of the three towns or book from San Sebastián.

Listings West of San Sebastián

Tourist information

Zarautz

Tourist office
Nafarroa Kalea 3, T943 830 990, www.turismozarautz.eus. Summer Mon-Sat 0900-2000, Sun 1000-1400, winter Mon-Fri 0930-1330, 1530-1900, Sat 1000-1400.
On a modern square on the main street through town.

Where to stay

Zarautz
See also Restaurants, below.

€€ Hotel Olatu
Ipar Kalea 10, T943 005 522, www.olatuhotela.com.
In the heart of the old town, this modern hotel makes a good base. Minimalist, compact rooms have a/c and it is a good deal. Some street noise at weekends and in summer.

Camping

Gran Camping Zarautz
T943 831 238, www.grancampingzarautz.com.
A massive campsite with the lot, open all year but packed in summer's dog days.

Getaria

€€ Hotel Itxas Gain
C San Roque 1, T943 141 035, www.hotelitxasgain.com.
Lovely place overlooking the sea (that's what the name means). This warm-hearted and open place has really lovely modernized rooms with arty touches. On the top floor there's a suite with a spa-bath. There's also a small clifftop garden, a top place to relax in hot weather. Recommended.

€€ Pensión Katrapona
Plaza Katrapona s/n, T943 140 409, www.katrapona.com.
Set in a great restored stone building tucked away behind the Mayflower restaurant, this

upmarket modern *pensión* has spotless and comfortable rooms with plenty of natural light and little balconies.

€ Gure Ametsa
Orrua s/n, T943 140 077,
www.nekatur.net/gureametsa.
Off a backroad between Zumaia and Getaria, this friendly, simple rural accommodation is in a superb location with hilly views over the sea. There are also cheaper rooms without en suite. Great value in summer.

Restaurants

Zarautz

€€€ Karlos Arguiñano
C Mendilauta 13, T943 130 000,
www.hotelka.com.
This is the lair of Spain's most famous TV chef, a cheerful fellow. Right on the beach, his restaurant, converted from a stone mansion, boasts high-class cuisine that's innovative without losing its local roots. There are also comfortable hotel rooms (€€€€) set in the tower of the building and great views over the beach from the castellated rooftop terrace.

€€ Kulixka
C Bixkonde 1, T943 134 604, www.kulixka.com.
A welcoming waterfront restaurant with an unbeatable view of the beach. There's good seafood, roast meats and a decent *menú del día*, as well as a night-time version for a few euros more.

Getaria
Getaria is well-stocked with restaurants serving fresh fish and the local *txakolí*, the best around.

€€€ Kaia-Kaipe
C Katrapona Aundia 10, T943 140 500,
www.kaia-kaipe.com.
The best and priciest of Getaria's restaurants with a sweeping view over the harbour and high standard of food and service. Whole fish

grilled over the coals outside are a highlight, as is the exceptional and reasonable wine list.

€€ Mayflower
C Katrapona 4, T943 140 658.
One of a number of *asadores*, right down by the port. Grilled sardines are a tasty speciality.

€€ Politena
Kale Nagusia 9, T943 140 113,
www.facebook.com/politena.getaria.
A bar oriented towards weekend visitors from Bilbao and San Sebastián. There's an enticing selection of *pintxos*, and good daily/weekend menus.

What to do

Getaria
Diving
K-Sub, *C Txoritonpe 34, T943 140 185, www.ksub.net.* Offers PADI scuba courses, hires out diving equipment and gives advice on good dive spots.

Transport

Orio and Zarautz
Bus
Buses run regularly to/from **San Sebastián** to Orio and Zarautz, and from Bilbao to Zarautz.

Train
Both Orio and Zarautz are serviced by **Euskotren** hourly from **Bilbao's** Atxuri station and **San Sebastián's** Amara station.

Getaria
Bus
Getaria is serviced by bus from **San Sebastián** regularly.

Train
Zumaia is serviced by **Euskotren** trains hourly from **Bilbao's** Atxuri station and **San Sebastián's** Amara station. Regular buses connect the 2 towns.

Vizcayan
Coast

The Vizcayan section of the Basque coastline is some of the most attractive and dramatic of Northern Spain: cliffs plunge into the water around tiny fishing villages, surfers ride impossibly long breaks, and the towns, like spirited Ondarroa, are home to a convivial and quintessentially Basque social scene. The eastern section is the most rough-edged, with stirring cliffs and startling geological folding contrasting with the green foliage. Fishing is god around here: some of the small villages are far more accessible by sea than by land. The main town of this stretch is the picturesque harbour settlement of Lekeitio, one of Euskadi's highlights.

riverside town with a strong Basque flavour

The friendliest of towns, Ondarroa marks the border of Vizcaya and Guipúzcoa. Situated at the mouth of the Río Artibai, the town is straddled by two bridges, one the harmonious stone Puente Viejo, the other a modern work by Santiago Calatrava, which sweeps across with unmistakable panache.

Although low on glamour and short on places to stay, Ondarroa could be worth a stop if you're exploring the coast, for its unpretentious Basque scene, working fishing fleet and small bars pumping with nationalist rock.

Markina-Xemein

This village in the Vizcayan hills, a short distance inland from Ondarroa, is set around a long leafy plaza. Not a great deal goes on here but what does is motivated by one thing and one thing only: *pelota* (see box, page 55). Many 'sons of Markina' have achieved star status in the sport, and the *frontón* is proudly dubbed the 'university of *pelota*'. As well as the more common *pelota a mano*, played with bare hands, there are regular games of *cesta punta*, in which a long wicker scoop is worn like a glove, adding some serious velocity to the game. Games are usually on a Sunday evening; check the website, www.euskalpilota.com – change to Spanish, go to the 'Cartelera' section, choose the date, leave the rest blank, and search (Buscar).

The hexagonal chapel of **San Miguel de Arretxinaga** is a 10-minute stroll from the plaza on the other side of the small river. The building itself is unremarkable but inside, surprisingly, are three enormous rocks, naturally balanced, with an altar to the saint underneath that far predates the building. According to local tradition, St Michael buried the devil here; a lingering odour of brimstone would tend to confirm this. This is the place to be at midnight on 29 September, when the village gathers to perform two traditional dances, the *aurresku* and the *mahai gaineko*.

Listings Ondarroa

Tourist information

Ondarroa tourist office
Erribera 9, near the old bridge, T946 831 951, turismobulegoa@ondarroakoudala.net. Mid-Sep to Jun Mon-Sat 1030-1330, 1700-1930, Sun 1030-1400, Jul to mid-Sep daily 1030-1400, 1630-1930.

Where to stay

€ Patxi
Arta Bide 21, T609 986 446, keitogabon@gmail.com.
On the sloping street heading down into the town when coming from the west,

this is a basic but exceedingly good-value *pensión* with comfortable rooms and a shared bathroom.

Markina Xemein

€ Intxauspe
Barrio Atxondo 10, T652 770 889, www.intxauspe.com.
Just north of the centre of Markina, this beautifully restored stone farmhouse is a *casa rural* that has a caring owner and 5 pretty, comfortable rooms, ideal for a relaxing stay in this corner of rural Vizcaya.

Restaurants

€€ Erretegia José Manuel
C Sabino Arana 23, T946 830 104.
Although it does a range of other appetizing dishes including tasty fresh fish, the big charcoal grill outside this restaurant caters to carnivores with large appetites. Forget quarter-pounders; here the steaks approach the kilogram mark (good for sharing) and are very juicy and tasty. Go for the *buey* (ox) for extra flavour.

€€ Sutargi
Nasa Kalea 11, T946 832 258, www.sutargi.com.
A popular bar with an excellent restaurant upstairs serving traditional Basque seafood specialities. Difficult to get a table at weekends.

Bars and clubs

Ondarroa's nightlife scene revolves around the main streets of the old centre. Nasa Kalea is well stocked with bars, many of which are temples to Basque rock, which is heavily identified with the independence movement.

Transport

Ondarroa is served by **Bizkaibus** from **Bilbao** bus station (half-hourly) via **Markina** and Lurraldebus from **San Sebastián** bus station (50 mins), 4 times a day (twice at weekends).

★ Lekeitio
charming medieval fishing town with excellent nearby beaches

Along the Basque coastline, Lekeitio stands out as one of the best places to visit and stay. Its fully functioning fishing harbour is full of cheerfully painted boats, and the tall old houses seem to be jostling and squeezing each other for a front-row seat. Once a favourite of holidaying royalty, the town is lively at weekends and in summer, when it's a popular destination for Bilbao and San Sebastián families. There are two beaches – the one a bit further from town, across the bridge, is better. Both look across to the pretty rocky islet of the Isla de San Nicolás in the middle of the bay, covered in trees and home only to seagulls. The countryside around Lekeitio is beautiful, with rolling hills and jagged cliffs. The emerald green colour unfortunately doesn't come for nothing though – the town gets its fair share of rainy days.

The narrow streets backing the harbour conceal a few well-preserved medieval buildings, while the harbour itself is lined with bars. As well as the lighthouse, with its display on navigation, the **Basílica de Santa María de la Asunción** is worth a visit. Lauded as one of the best examples of Basque Gothic architecture, it seems to change colour completely from dull grey to warm orange depending on the light. The *retablo* is an ornate piece of Flemish work, while the exterior has extravagant flying buttresses.

Elantxobe

If tiny fishing villages are your thing, Elantxobe, west of Lekeitio, might be worth adding to your itinerary. With amazingly steep and narrow streets leading down to a small harbour, it seems a forgotten place, tucked away at the bottom of a sheer escarpment. It's authentic without being overly picturesque. There's now a road that winds around the hill down to the port, but the bus still gets spun around on a turntable in the tiny square up above. There are a few places to try the catch of the day, and simple lodgings. **Bizkaibus**

A3513 between Bilbao and Lekeitio stops here. It leaves Bilbao every two hours from Calle Hurtado Amezaga by Abando train station.

Beyond Elantxobe, the coast is broken by the **Urdaibai estuary**, home to many waterbirds. The good beach of **Laia** looks across at the surfing village of **Mundaka**, but the road heads a fair way inland, crossing the river at the area's main town, Gernika.

Listings Lekeitio

Tourist information

Lekeitio tourist office
C Independencia s/n, T946 844 017, turismo@lekeitio.eus. Tue-Sun 1000-1400, summer daily 1000-1500, 1600-1900.
Has a good range of information.

Where to stay

€€€ Hotel Palacio Oxangoiti
Gamarra Kalea 2, T944 650 555, www.oxangoiti.net.
This loving conversion of a 17th-century palace in the heart of town will win you over with its friendly welcome and elegant old-style decor. It's an intimate place with just 7 rooms (the bathrooms are gleamingly modern), so you'll need to book ahead.

€€ Hotel Zubieta
Portal de Atea, T946 843 030, www.hotelzubieta.com.
A superbly converted coachhouse in the grounds of a *palacio*. With surprisingly low prices, this is one of the best places to stay, with friendly management, a lively bar, and cosy rooms with sloping wooden ceilings. Recommended.

Elantxobe

€ Itsasmin Ostatua
C Nagusia 32, T946 276 174, www.itsasmin.com.
This spruce place has bags of charm. Some rooms have lovely views down over the cascading village to the port below.

Restaurants

Despite the busy summer scene, there are lots of fairly traditional places to eat and drink.

€€ Egaña
C Antiguako Ama 2, T946 840 103, www.eganarestaurante.com.
Attractive traditional restaurant, which stands out for its warm personal service and good selection of fresh fish.

€ Lumentza
C Buenaventura Zapirain 3, T946 841 501, www.lumentza.com.
This local favourite is a modern backstreet *pintxo* bar decked out with warm lighting and blond wood. The snacks are based on traditional good quality rather than avant-garde invention and are delicious. There's a stool-and-banquette area out the back for a sit-down meal.

Bars and clubs

Talako Bar
Above the fisherman's cooperative on the harbour.
A great spot for one of Lekeitio's rainy days, with a pool table, board games and a 180° view of the harbour, town and beaches.

Festivals

5 Sep Fiesta de San Antolín. In a land of strange festivals, this is one of the strangest. It involves a long rope, a few rowing boats, plenty of able-bodied young folk and a (dead) goose. The hapless bird is tied in the middle of the rope, stretched across the harbour. Competitors take turns from rowing boats to grab the goose's head (which has been liberally greased up). The rope is then tightened, lifting the grabber into the air, and then slackened, dunking them in the water. This is repeated until either the goose's head comes off, or the person falls off.

Transport

Bizkaibus hourly from the bus station in **Bilbao** (1 hr 15 mins), **Lurraldebus** 4 a day from the bus station in **San Sebastián** (2 at weekends, 1 hr 25 mins).

★ Guernica/Gernika

thriving modern town, a symbol of Basque culture and identity

A name that weighs on the tongue, heavy with blood and atrocity, is Gernika, but this thriving town and symbol of Basque pride and nationalism has moved on from its tragic past, and provides the visitor with a great opportunity to experience Basque culture.

Today, Gernika is anything but a sombre memorial to the devastation it suffered (see box, opposite). While it understandably lacks much of its original architecture, it's a happy and friendly place that merits a visit. The Monday morning market is entertaining to check out.

Casa de Juntas
Open 1000-1400, 1600-1800 (1900 in summer), free.

The Casa de Juntas, symbolically placed next to the famous oak tree, is once again the seat of the Vizcayan parliament. The highlight of the building itself is the room with a massive stained-glass roof depicting the oak tree. The tree itself is outside by the porch, while part of the trunk of an older one is enshrined in a slightly silly little pavilion.

Parque de los Pueblos de Europa
Behind the Casa de Juntas, 1000-1900 (2100 summer).

This park contains sculptures by Henry Moore and Eduardo Chillida. Both recall the devastated buildings of the town and are dedicated to peace.

Museo de la Paz
Plaza Foru 1, T946 270 213, www.museodelapaz.org. Mar-Sep Tue-Sat 1000-1900, Sun 1000-1400, Oct-Feb Tue-Sat 1000-1400, 1600-1800, Sun 1000-1400, closed Jan. €5.

Gernika's showpiece, the Museo de la Paz (Museum of Peace), is an excellent and moving museum. It focuses on peace as a concept and as a goal to strive for, examines the Gernika bombing, then, crucially, the importance of reconciliation and an optimistic outlook. Two excellent audiovisual presentations are included; the staff cleverly put these in the right language as they monitor your progress through the museum. A visit to Gernika is highly recommended for this museum alone.

Euskal Herria Museoa
C Allende Salazar 5, T946 255 451, Tue-Sat 1000-1400, 1600-1900, Sun 1030-1430, €3.

Housed in a strikingly beautiful 18th-century *palacio*, this museum is the repository for a sizeable collection of artefacts relating to the history and ethnography of the Basque Country.

ON THE ROAD
The bombing of Gernika

During the Spanish Civil War, in one of the most despicable planned acts of modern warfare there has been, 59 German and Italian planes destroyed the town in a bombardment that lasted three gruelling hours. It was 26 April 1937, and market day in Gernika, thousands of villagers from the surrounding area were in the town, which had no air defences to call on. Three days earlier a similar bombardment had killed over 250 in the town of Durango and they came again here. Splinter and incendiary bombs were used for maximum impact, and fighters strafed fleeing people with machine guns. The casualty figures are a matter of debate – different versions put the figure anywhere from 150 to 1700.

Franco, the head of the Nationalist forces, simply denied the event had occurred; he claimed that any damage had been caused by Basque propagandists. In 1999 Germany formally apologized for the event, making the Spanish conspicuous by their silence. Apart from a general wish to terrorize and subdue the Basque population, who were resisting the Nationalist advance on Bilbao, Gernika's symbolic value was important. For many centuries Basque assemblies had met here under an oak tree – this was common to many Vizcayan towns, but the Gernika meetings became dominant. They were attended by the monarch or a representative, who would swear to respect Basque rights and laws – the *fueros*. Thus the town became a powerful symbol of Basque liberty and nationhood. The first modern Basque government, a product of the Civil War, was sworn in under the oak only six months before the bombing.

One of the most famous results of the bombing was Picasso's painting, named after the town. He had been commissioned by the Republican government to paint a mural for the upcoming World Fair, and this was the result. It currently sits in the Reina Sofía gallery in Madrid although constant Basque lobbying may yet bring it to Bilbao. A ceramic copy has been made on a wall on Calle Allende Salazar in Gernika itself. Picasso commented on his painting: "By means of it, I express my abhorrence of the race that sunk Spain in an ocean of pain and death".

Listings Guernica/Gernika

Tourist information

Gernika tourist office
Artekale 8, T946 255 892, turismo@gernika-lumo.net. Nov-Easter Mon-Fri 1000-1800, Sat-Sun 1000-1400, Easter-Oct Mon-Sat 1000-1900, Sun 1000-1400.
Guided tours of the town leave here daily at 1100. English-speaking staff.

Where to stay

€€ Hotel Katxi
Morga/Andra Mari s/n, T946 270 740, www.katxi.com.
A few kilometres west of Gernika in the hamlet of Morga is this excellent rural hotel. The rooms, some larger than others, are extremely comfortable, and there's a friendly lounge area. It's a great place to get away, with a warm atmosphere, and plenty of opportunity for relaxing on the terrace or in

the garden. The owners run a good *asador* next door. Recommended.

€€-€ Akelarre Ostatua
C Barrenkale 5, T946 270 197, www.hotelakelarre.com.
This enjoyable place has funky little rooms with TV and varnished floorboards. There's a terrace to take some sun and it's in the heart of the pedestrian area. There are discounts if you stay more than 1 night, and it's significantly cheaper off-season. If there's nobody there, you can access and pay via a computer terminal.

Restaurants

€€ Zallo Barri
Juan Calzada Kalea 79, T946 251 800, www.zallobarri.com.
Locals in the know will tell you that this is Gernika's best value place to eat. It's about a 15-min walk south of the centre but worth every stride. Crisp white linen and elegant glassware create an ambience that is upheld by the quality Basque cuisine and welcoming service.

Bars and clubs

Arrano
C Juan Calzada 6, www.facebook.com/gernikako.arranotaberna.
A vibrant Basque bar with a lively young crowd spilling outside at weekends.

Transport

There are hourly trains to Gernika from **Bilbao**'s Atxuri station, and buses ½ hourly (hourly at weekends) from C Hurtado de Amezaga next to Abando station (30 mins).

Around Gernika

area of natural beauty, a haven for wildlife

Urdaibai Reserve
Gernika sits at the head of the estuary of the Río Oka, the Urdaibai Reserve, a varied area of tidal sandflats and riverbank ecology that is home to a huge amount of wildlife. UNESCO declared it a Biosphere Reserve in 1984. It's a great spot for birdwatching, but mammals such as the badger, marten and wild boar are also present.

The **park headquarters** ⓘ *T946 257 125*, are on the edge of the town centre of Gernika in the Palacio de Udetxea on the far side of the Parque de los Pueblos. Vistas of the estuary can be had from either side of the estuary, but to really appreciate the area, you might be better off taking a tour.

Cueva de Santimamiñe
Kortezubi, www.santimamine.com. Tours cost €5 and are limited to 20 people on a first-come, first-served basis so should be booked ahead by phone T944 651 657, or email santimamine@bizkaia.net. They run Easter to mid-Oct daily 1000, 1100, 1200, 1300, 1530, 1700, 1730, mid-Oct to Easter Tue-Sun 1000, 1100, 1200, 1300. The visit lasts about 90 mins.

The cave of Santimamiñe was an elegant and spacious home for thousands of generations of prehistoric folk, who decorated it with an important series of paintings depicting bison, among other animals. Apart from the entrance chamber, the cave is now closed to the public to protect the paintings and allow ongoing archaeological investigation, but it's still worth booking a guided visit. Starting with a stroll through the holm-oak hillside, you then visit the cave entrance and end up in an interpretation centre where you embark on a virtual visit of the entire cave while wearing 3D specs. Apart from the paintings, you

Cod, whales and America

In former times whales were a common species off the northern coast of Spain. The Basques were hunting them as far back as the seventh century. It became a major enterprise and, as the whales grew scarcer, they had to venture far into the North Atlantic. It's a good bet they reached America in the 14th century at the latest, signing the native Americans' visitors' book under the Vikings and the shadowy, debatable scrawl of St Brendan.

The whaling expeditions provisioned themselves by fishing and preserving cod. The folk back home got a taste for this *bacalao*, and they still love it. Meanwhile, Elkano became the first man to circumnavigate the globe, after the expedition leader, Magellan, was killed in the Philippines. Basque whalers established many settlements along the coast of Labrador during the 16th century and, later, Basques left their homes in droves for the promise of the New World; Basque culture has been significant in the development of the USA, particularly in some of the western states, as well as in Argentina and Chile.

---

see the eerily beautiful rock formations. The bus from Gernika to Lekeitio (approximately every two hours) can drop you at the turn-off just before the town of Kortezubi. From there it's a half-hour walk.

Bosque Pintado de Oma
www.bosquedeoma.com. Free.

Near the caves is an unusual artwork: the Bosque Pintado de Oma. In a peaceful pine forest on a ridge, artist Agustín Ibarrola has painted eyes, people and geometric figures on the tree trunks in bright, bold colours. Some of the trees combine to form larger pictures – these can be difficult to make out, and it doesn't help that most of the display panels have been erased. Overall, it's a tranquil place with the wind whispering through the pines, and there's a strangely primal quality about the work. It's hard not to feel that more could have been made of the original concept though. A dirt track climbs 3 km to the wood from opposite the **Lezika** restaurant next to the Santimamiñe caves. It's a pleasant walk, and if it's a nice day, it's worth returning another way. Take the path down the hill at the other end of the Bosque from the entrance. After crossing a couple of fields, you'll find yourself in the tiny hamlet of **Oma**, with attractive Basque farmhouses. Turning left along the road will lead you back to the caves.

Listings Around Gernika

Restaurants

€€ Lezika
Cuevas de Santimamiñe, Kortezubi,
T946 252 975, www.restaurantelezika.com.

The whole of Vizcaya seems to descend on the beer garden here at weekends with kids and dogs in tow; the restaurant is worthwhile as well and better value than the *raciones* on offer at the bar.

laid-back surf mecca and a bustling fishing town

From Gernika, following the west bank of the estuary takes you back to the coast. A brisk half-hour's walk is all that separates the fishing towns of Bermeo and Mundaka, but they couldn't be more different. Mundaka is petite and slightly upmarket as visitors come to admire its beautiful harbour. Bermeo puts it in the shade in fishing terms: as one of the most important ports on this coast some of its boats seem bigger than Mundaka's harbour. There's a good atmosphere though, and an attractive old town.

Mundaka

While Mundaka still has its small fishing fleet, it's better known as a surfing village. It's a mecca of the global surf community, with a magnificent left-break (a wave that breaks from right to left, looking towards the beach). When the wind blows and the big waves roll in, a good surfer can jump in off the rocks by Mundaka harbour and ride a wave right across the estuary mouth to Laida beach, a couple of kilometres away. Even if catching waves isn't your thing, Mundaka is still well worth visiting, with a beautiful bonsai harbour and relaxed ambience. The village is a small maze of winding streets and an oversized church. There are some good places to stay or camp, and it's within striking distance of several highlights of the Basque coast. In summer, boats run across to **Laida beach**, which is the best in the area. The town's surf shop, www.mundakasurfshop.com, is the place to go for equipment and advice.

Bermeo

Bermeo is a bigger and more typical Basque fishing town with a more self-sufficient feel. One of the whaling towns that more or less pioneered the activity on this coast, Bermeo has a proud maritime history documented in its museum. The ships for Columbus's second voyage were built and largely crewed from here. There's much more action in the fishing harbour here than in peaceful Mundaka.

The old town is worth a visit. There's a cobbled square across which the church and the Ayuntamiento vie for power; the latter has a sundial on its face. There's a small chunk of the old town wall preserved, with a symbolic footprint of John the Baptist, who is said to have made modern triple jumpers weep by leaping from here to the sanctuary of Gaztelugatxe in three steps. The **Museo del Pescador (Arrantzaleen Museoa)** ⓘ *Plaza Torrontero 1, T946 881 171, Tue-Sat 1000-1400, 1600-1900, Sun 1000-1400, €3*, is set in a 15th-century tower and is devoted to the Basque fishing industry. The tourist office is opposite the station.

If you want to get out on the water, **Hegaluze** ⓘ *T666 791 021, www.hegaluze.com*, runs coastal trips, whale- and dolphin-watching excursions, and cruises in the Urdaibai estuary in a small covered boat.

Santuario de San Juan de Gaztelugatxe and around

West of Bermeo, some 6 km from town, is the spectacular sanctuary of San Juan de Gaztelugatxe. In the early 11th century, Sancho the Great, King of Navarra, was in Aquitaine, in France, when a surprising gift was presented to the local church hierarchy: the head of John the Baptist, which had mysteriously turned up a short while before. As a result, the cult of the Baptist received an understandable boost and many monasteries and sanctuaries were built in his name, including several in northeastern Spain, with the express encouragement of the impressed Sancho.

San Juan de Gaztelugatxe is one of these (although the church dates from much later). A rocky island frequently rendered impressively bleak by the coastal squalls, is connected by a bridge to the mainland, from where it's 231 steps to the top. Apart from the view, there's not a great deal to see, but the setting is spectacular. The island is a pilgrimage spot, particularly for the feast of St John on 24 June, and also on 31 July. To get there from Bermeo, take a bus (about every two hours) along the coast road towards Bakio; you can get off opposite the sanctuary. While you're here, have lunch at the Eneperi, overlooking the sanctuary with a superb terrace, cheap lunches and *pintxos* in the bar, an excellent, more upmarket, restaurant, and even a small museum.

Listings Mundaka and Bermeo

Tourist information

Mundaka

Tourist office
Kepa Deuna s/n, T946 177 201, turismo.
mundaka@bizkaia.org. Tue-Sat 1030-1330
and 1600-1900, Sun 1100-1400.
Small office near Mundaka's harbour.

Where to stay

Mundaka

€€€ Hotel Atalaya
C Itxaropen 1, T946 177 000,
www.atalayahotel.es.
The classiest of the town's options, with a summery feel to its rooms and café. Garden and parking adjoin the stately building. Great breakfasts (not included) and excellent service.

€€ Hotel El Puerto
Portu Kalea 1, T946 876 725,
www.hotelelpuerto.com.
The best value of Mundaka's 3 hotels, set right by the tiny fishing harbour. Delightful rooms, very cosy and some overlooking the harbour (worth paying the few extra euros). The bar below is one of Mundaka's best but noise can carry to the rooms above it. Recommended.

€€ Hotel Mundaka
C Florentino Larrinaga 9, T946 876 700,
www.hotelmundaka.com.
This well-cared for hotel offers rather pleasant rooms just back from the water, with plenty of space and comfortable beds. There's also a garden and café-bar.

Camping

Portuondo
1 km out of Mundaka on the road to Gernika,
T946 877 701, www.campingportuondo.com.
Sardined during the summer, this is a well-equipped campsite with a pool, cafés and laundry. There are bungalows (a week minimum stay in summer) that sleep up to 4, but are not significantly cheaper than the hotels in town if you're only 2. They do come with kitchen, fridge and television though.

Bermeo

There are good rural tourism options in the hills behind Bermeo.

€€ Hostal Torre Ercilla
C Talaranzko 14, T946 187 598,
torrercilla@euskalnet.net.
A lovely place to stay in Bermeo's old town, between the museum and church. Rooms are designed for relaxation, with small balconies, reading nooks and soft carpet. Don't worry about losing your key; access to your room is via fingerprint scan.

Restaurants

Mundaka

€€€ Restaurante Portuondo
T946 876 050, www.restaurante
portuondo.com.
About 1.5 km south of central Mundaka, this
excellent place has sweet views over the
estuary and a great line in grilled meat and
fish. Recommended.

Transport

Hourly trains to both towns from **Bilbao**'s
Atxuri station, and ½-hourly buses from C
Hurtado de Amezaga next to Abando station.

Vitoria/
Gasteiz

Vitoria (with a population of around 244,000) is the quiet achiever of the trio of Basque cities. As it's a comparatively quiet, tranquil town, it comes as a surprise to many visitors to discover that it's actually the capital of the semi-autonomous Basque region. A thoughtful place, it combines an attractive old town with an Ensanche (expansion) designed to provide plenty of green spaces for its hard-working inhabitants. While it lacks the big-city vitality of Bilbao or the languid beauty of San Sebastián it's a satisfying city much loved by most who visit it. Perhaps because it's the political centre of the region, the young are very vocally Basque, and the city feels energized as a result. An ambitious urban improvement plan has brought ongoing improvements to the city.

Calle Cuchillería and Calle Chiquita

Calle Cuchillería, and its continuation, Calle Chiquita, is the liveliest part of the old town, with several impressive old mansions, a couple of museums, dozens of bars, and plenty of pro-Basque political attitude. Indeed, there's an interesting contrast in the atmosphere of the new and old towns; whereas the former feels very Spanish and quite staid, the preserve of middle-aged strollers, the old streets hum with young Basque energy. Like several in the Casco Medieval, this street is named after the craftspeople who used to have shops here; in this case knife makers. Walking along this street and those nearby you can see a number of old inscriptions and coats of arms carved on buildings.

Housed in a beautiful fortified medieval house on Cuchillería with a sleek modern extension out the back **Bibat** ⓘ *Tue-Fri 1000-1400, 1600-1830, Sat 1000-1400, Sun 1100-1400, €3*, contains two museums. The unusual Fournier collection is devoted to the playing card, of which it holds over 10,000 packs. Diamonds are forever, but you won't see many here: the cards are mostly Spanish decks, with swords, cups, coins and staves the suits. Here also is the archaeology museum. The province has been well occupied over history, and the smallish collection covers many periods, from prehistoric through Roman and medieval. Arguably the most impressive of the objects on display is the *Knight's Stele*, a tombstone carved with a horseman dating from the Roman era.

The corner of the old town at the end of Calle Chiquita is one of Vitoria's most picturesque. **El Portalón**, now a restaurant, is a lovely old timbered building from the late 15th century. It used to be an inn and a staging post for messengers. Across from it is the **Torre de los Anda**, which defended one of the entrances in the city wall. Opposite these is the 16th-century house of the Gobeo family.

Opposite here is the current entrance to the older of Vitoria's two cathedrals, the **Catedral de Santa María** ⓘ *tours daily 1000-1400, 1600-1900, €8.50 per person, pre-book on T945 255 135 or www.catedralvitoria.com*. There's an ongoing restoration project, but it's currently 'open for renovation'; while normal visits have been suspended, you can take a fascinating guided tour of the restoration works.

Above the busy square of **Plaza de la Virgen Blanca**, the church of **San Miguel** stands like one of a series of chess pieces guarding the entrance to the Casco Medieval. Two gaping arches mark the portal, which is superbly carved. A niche here holds the city's patron saint, the Virgen Blanca, a coloured late-Gothic figure. The

Essential Vitoria/Gasteiz

Finding your feet

Vitoria is a good two-wheel city with more cycle ways and green spots than in busier Bilbao. There's a relatively new tram line, but Vitoria is easily walkable with Calle Dato the focus of the evening *paseo*. The new bus station is on the northern side of town, with tram access to/from the centre.

When to go

The city comes alive during the Fiesta de la Virgen Blanca in August, but make sure you reserve your accommodation and train tickets well in advance.

Time required

Give yourself a day and a half for the main sights, and two nights to enjoy the quality restaurant scene.

BACKGROUND
Vitoria/Gasteiz

Vitoria's shield-shaped old town sits on the high ground that perhaps gave the city its name (*beturia* is an Euskara word for hill). After being a Basque settlement first, then a Roman one, Vitoria was abandoned until it was refounded and fortified by the kings of Navarra in the 12th and 13th centuries. An obscure Castilian town for much of its history, Vitoria featured in the Peninsular War, when, on midsummer's day in 1813, Napoleon's forces were routed by the Allied troops and fled in ragged fashion towards home, abandoning their baggage train containing millions of francs, which was gleefully looted. "The battle was to the French", commented a British officer sagely, "like salt on a leech's tail". Vitoria has thrived since being named capital of the semi-autonomous Basque region, and has a genteel, comfortable air, enlivened by an active student population.

saint's day is 5 August, and on the 4th, a group of townspeople carry the figure of Celedón (a stylized farmer) from the top of the graceful belltower down to the square.

Los Arquillos

Running off the same square, this slightly strange series of dwellings and covered colonnades was designed in the early 19th century as a means of more effectively linking the high Casco Medieval with the newer town below, and to avoid the risk of the collapse of the southern part of the hill. It leads up to the attractive small **Plaza del Machete**, where incoming city chancellors used to swear an oath of allegiance over a copy of the Fueros (exemptions from royal taxes) and a *machete*, in this case a military cutlass.

Also off Plaza de la Virgen Blanca, the picture-postcard **Plaza de España** (Basques prefer to call it **Plaza Nueva**) was designed by the same man, Olaguíbel, who thought up the Arquillos. It's a beautiful colonnaded square busy with playing children and parents chatting over coffee, housing the town hall and several bars with terraces that are perfect for the morning or afternoon sun.

New Town

attractive green spaces and a top art gallery

Vitoria's new town isn't going to blow anyone's mind with a cavalcade of Gaudí-esque buildings or wild street parties, but it is a very satisfying place: a planned mixture of attractive streets and plenty of parkland. It's got the highest amount of greenery per citizen of any city in Spain and it's no surprise that it's been voted one of the best places to live in the country. With the innovative Artium adding a touch of original, the mantle of Basque capital seems to sit ever easier on Vitoria's shoulders.

Artium

C Francia 24, T945 209 020, www.artium.org, Tue-Fri 1100-1400, 1700-2000, Sat-Sun 1100-2000, €6, Wed name your price.

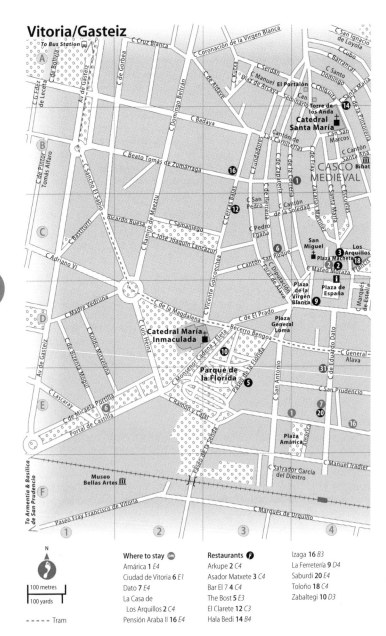

Vitoria/Gasteiz

Where to stay

América 1 E4
Ciudad de Vitoria 6 E1
Dato 7 E4
La Casa de
 Los Arquillos 2 C4
Pensión Araba II 16 E4

Restaurants

Arkupe 2 C4
Asador Matxete 3 C4
Bar El 7 4 C4
The Bost 5 E3
El Clarete 12 C3
Hala Bedi 14 B4

Izaga 16 B3
La Ferretería 9 D4
Saburdi 20 E4
Toloño 18 C4
Zabaltegi 10 D3

Artium is Vitoria's answer to Bilbao's Guggenheim and San Sebastián's Kursaal. It's an exciting project that features some excellent contemporary artwork, mostly in the form of temporary exhibitions, some of which incorporate some of the older buildings in Vitoria's Casco Medieval. Shiny and white, your attention is grabbed immediately by the building's confident angles and Javier Pérez's *Un pedazo de cielo cristalizado* (A piece of sky made glass), a large hanging-glass sculpture in the atrium. The galleries are accessed down the stairs. The website has details in English about what's on at any given time; the exhibitions are usually in place for many months. There's also a good little café.

Catedral de María Inmaculada

There's no missing the new cathedral, María Inmaculada, constructed in the 20th century in neo-Gothic style; its bulk looms attractively over this part of the town. Built in medieval style, it now houses the **Museo Diocesano de Arte Sacro** ① *Tue-Fri 1100-1400, 1600-1830, Sat 1000-1400, Sun 1100-1400, €3.*

Parque de la Florida

This gorgeous park is an excellent retreat right in the heart of Vitoria. Cool and shady, it has a number of exotic trees and plants and a couple of peaceful cafés. You can watch old men in berets playing *bolas* (boules), and there's an old bandstand with Sunday concerts, guarded by statues of four ancient kings. If you see anyone taking life a little too seriously, they're more than likely politicians – the Basque Parliament stands in a corner of the park.

Basílica de San Prudencio

Currently only open before Mass Tue-Sat 1900, Sun 1200 and 1300, though you may find it open at other times.

It's well worth the half-hour walk or the bus ride to see this church in the village of **Armentia**, now subsumed into Vitoria's outskirts. The village is supposedly the birthplace of San Prudencio, the patron saint of Alava province, and the church was erected in his honour. It was rebuilt in the 18th century, but still has some excellent features from its Romanesque youth, such as a harmonious round apse and the carvings above the doors, one of Christ and the apostles, the other of the Lamb and John the Baptist. Check visiting status with the tourist office before setting out, as access to the interior depends on the renovation works.

To reach Armentia on foot, continue past the Museo de Bellas Artes on Paseo Fray Francisco de Vitoria, then turn left down Paseo de Cervantes when you reach the modern chapel of **La Sagrada Familia**. The basilica is at the end of this road. It's a pleasant walk; you can also get bus No 4, which runs every 10 minutes from the new cathedral to the basilica.

Anillo Verde
Vitoria has been developing a reputation as a park city, and this excellent initiative is part of that. The 'Green Ring' runs for 30 km around the city, connecting various parks and the Salburua wetlands via a cyclable and walkable trail. Salburua, a good birdwatching spot, is a good place to start, because you can borrow bikes and binoculars at the Ataria visitor centre ① *Paseo de la Biosfera 4, T945 254 759, www.vitoria-gasteiz.org/ataria, Oct-Apr Tue-Fri 1100-1400, 1600-1900, Sat-Sun 1100-1400, 1600-1900, May-Sep Tue-Fri 1100-1400, 1600-2000, Sat-Sun 1100-1400, 1600-2000,* here. There's an app you can download with details and directions too.

Listings Vitoria/Gasteiz *map page 100.*

Tourist information

Vitoria tourist office
In the centre, Plaza España 1, T945 161 598, turismo@vitoria-gasteiz.org. Jul-Sep daily 1000-2000, Oct-Jun Mon-Sat 1000-1900, Sun 1100-1400.

Where to stay

€€€ La Casa de los Arquillos
Paseo los Arquillos 1, T945 151 259, www.lacasadelosarquillos.com.
Very central, but in a quiet, charming nook of the old town, this is an excellent choice. Rooms are compact but artfully decorated with exposed stone and dashing contemporary whites and blacks. Larger 'lofts' are apartments with kitchen, available in a building a couple of blocks up the street.

€€€ Parador de Argómaniz
Carretera N1 Km 363, T945 293 200, www.parador.es.

This parador is some 12 km east of Vitoria in a Renaissance palace. It's a tranquil place with some good views over the surrounding countryside. Napoleon slept here before the disastrous Battle of Vitoria.

€€€-€€ Hotel Ciudad de Vitoria
Portal de Castilla 8, T945 141 100, www.hoteles-silken.com.
A massive 4-star hotel situated at the edge of Vitoria's centre, where character starts to make way for 'lifestyle'. It's airy and pleasant, with good facilities, including a gym and sauna. There are excellent off-season and weekend rates.

€€ Hotel Amárica
C Florida 11, T945 130 506, www.hotelamarica.com.
Just around the corner from C Dato and close to the train station, this friendly hotel is very well placed. The rooms are good value, with TV and good bathroom, warm, and surprisingly quiet, considering it's a busy street.

€€ Hotel Dato
C Eduardo Dato 28, T945 147 230,
www.hoteldato.com.
This *pintxo*-zone cheap hotel is a treasury
of art nouveau and classic statues, mirrors
and general plushness, in a comfortable
rather than stuffy way. Its small rooms are
exceptional value too; all are pretty, with
excellent facilities, and some have balconies
or miradors (enclosed balconies).

€ Pensión Araba II
C Florida 25, T945 232 588,
www.pensionaraba.com.
This elegant home makes an excellent
base in central Vitoria. A variety of spotless,
comfortable rooms with or without
bathroom and a genuinely friendly
welcome make it a budget star. Parking
spaces available (€6).

Restaurants

In the old town, C Cuchillería is a long row
of simple Basque taverns; smarter places
dot the new town, particularly around
C Eduardo Dato.

€€€ Arkupe
C Mateo Moraza 13, T945 230 080,
www.restaurantearkupe.com.
On the edge of the old town, this quality
restaurant turns out imaginative dishes that
are typically combinations of various quality
northern Spanish products. Try the juicy
carrilleras stewed in local Rioja, the range
of gourmet salads, or, on Thu, a traditional
cocido stew. The lively *pintxo* bar downstairs
is buzzy and worthwhile too.

€€ Asador Matxete
Plaza Machete 4, T945 131 821,
www.matxete.com.
This stylish, friendly restaurant is
harmoniously inserted into this pretty plaza
above Los Arquillos. The vaulted dining area
is atmospheric, and dishes such as quail
salad back up the excellent charcoal-grilled

meat, though service is a little patchy.
There's also a quality downstairs tapas bar
and pleasant terrace to enjoy a drink in this
peaceful square.

€€ El Clarete
C Cercas Bajas 18, T945 263 874,
www.elclareterestaurante.com.
Comfortably contemporary in style, this
enthusiastically run restaurant offers
confidently prepared modern Spanish
cuisine with an experimental flair. Portions,
while not huge, are beautifully presented
and taste fabulous: try the slow-roasted lamb
or anything with their home-made foie.

€€ Izaga
Tomás de Zumárraga 2, T945 138 200,
www.restauranteizaga.com.
Excellent dining at this fairly formal
restaurant in a smart stone building. The
focus is on seafood – try the delicious Huelva
prawns – but there are plenty of other
specialities – such as duck's liver on stuffed
pig's ear, and some sinful desserts.

€€ The Bost
C Florida 5, T945 131 248, www.thebost.es.
Casual dining with high quality and
generously low prices make this charismatic
place by the Florida park a winner. It's run
by the former owners of a legendary Vitoria
restaurant and offers 2 menus, one of tapas-
style plates, the other of fuller meals (or 'The
Bost' options, which feed a whole table).
Recommended.

€€ Toloño
Cuesta San Francisco 3, T945 233 336,
www.tolonobar.com.
One of the city's best *pintxo* bars, this smart
spot on the hill leading up to the old town
is a kidney-shaped space with an upbeat
and welcoming feel. The tapas are great,
especially the gourmet *pintxos* chalked
up on the board. For around €3, take your
pick from a range of exquisite hot delights;
the foie is great if it's on. Recommended.

€ Bar El 7
C Cuchillería 7, T945 272 298.
A Vitoria classic, this is an excellent bar at the head of the Casco Medieval's liveliest street. Its big range of *bocadillos* keeps students and all-comers happy. Order a half if you're not starving; they make 'em pretty large. They also do a very acceptable *menú del día*.

€ Hala Bedi
C Cuchillería 98, T945 260 411, www.halabedi.eus.
A late-opening Basque bar with a cheerful atmosphere. It's very lively, and popular with the young and politically conscious. Out of a tiny kitchen come crêpes with a massive variety of sweet and savoury fillings, as well as sandwiches and other simple dishes.

€ Saburdi
C Eduardo Dato 32, T945 147 016, www.saburdi.com.
There are some excellent *pintxo* bars in Vitoria, and this is one of the classics, with a great range of delicious bites. It's warmly lit and welcoming, with several decent wines by the glass. Recommended.

Cafés

La Ferretería
Plaza de la Virgen Blanca s/n, T945 133 922.
In the heart of Vitoria, this trendily lit former ironmongers is not to be sneered at if you're on the prowl for a morning coffee and croissant. If you grab a spot on its terrace in the early evening you can truly say you are sitting where it's all happening.

Zabaltegi
Parque de la Florida, www.zabaltegi.org.
One of Vitoria's best locations, with lots of tables among the trees of this peaceful park. Regular games of *bolas* take place nearby.

The old town tends to have boisterous, no-frills bars with a Basque atmosphere, while the new town has a more chic scene.

Bar Río
C Eduardo Dato 20, T945 230 067, www.riogasteiz.com.
A decent café with outdoor tables by day, and one of the last bars to shut at night, when it caters to a good-natured gay/straight crowd. They prepare mixed drinks with an unbelievably elaborate ritual.

Café Iguana
Correría 94, T945 122 837, www.facebook.com/iguanakafe.
This spot has a great ambience for an after-dinner *copa* and a friendly mix of arty people. Plenty of tables and well-mixed drinks. One of Vitoria's best.

El Bodegón de Gorbea
C Herrería 26.
A classic. No-frills bar with rock music, cheap beer, sociable outdoor terrace and a bohemian bunch of friendly Basques chatting and drinking from early until very late. On the corner of Cantón San Roque.

Festivals

25 Jul Santiago's day is celebrated as the **Día del Blusa**, when colour-coordinated kids patrol the streets.
4-9 Aug **Fiesta de la Virgen Blanca**, the city's major knees-up, is recommended.
Dec **Advent**. Vitoria is known for its spectacular life-sized Nativity scene (*Belén*), with over 200 figures.

Transport

Air
Vitoria's airport (VIT) is 8 km northwest of town. At time of research it was only used for cargo and charter flights.

Bus

The new bus station is on the northern side of town, with tram access to/from the centre. Buses to **Bilbao** run about every 30 mins with **Autobuses La Unión** (55 mins). There are 7-8 buses a day to **San Sebastián** (1 hr 40 mins), to **Madrid** (5 hrs), **Burgos** (1½ hrs), **Pamplona** (9-14 daily, 1 hr 40 mins), as well as buses to **Logroño**, **Haro**, **Laguardia**, and **Salvatierra**.

Train

Vitoria's **RENFE** station has better connections with the rest of Spain than does Bilbao. There are regular connections with **Madrid**, **Zaragoza**, **Logroño**, **Barcelona**, **Burgos**, and other destinations.

Tram

Vitoria's smart tram line crosses the city centre and costs €1.40 for a ride. It's mostly useful for getting between the centre and the bus station.

Alava
Province

The province of Alava is something of a wilderness compared to the densely settled valleys of Vizcaya and Guipúzcoa. It's the place to come for unspoiled nature; there are some spots of great natural beauty and plenty of scope for hiking and other more specialized outdoor activities. The attractive walled town of Salvatierra is worth a visit and a base for exploring the area. The southern part of the province drops away to sunny plains, part of the Rioja wine region. Laguardia, the area's main centre, is not to be missed.

Western Alava
an ancient cultural landscape and Spain's highest waterfall

West of Vitoria the green pastures give way to a rugged and dry terrain, home of vultures, eagles and dramatic rock formations. The area is served by bus from Vitoria.

Salinas de Añana
This hard-bitten half-a-horse village has one of the more unusual sights in the Basque lands. The place owes its existence to the incredibly saline water that wells up from the ground here, which was diverted down a valley and siphoned into any number of *eras* or pans, flat evaporation platforms mounted on wooded stilts. It's something very different and an eerie sight, looking a little like the ruins of an ancient Greek city in miniature. As many as 5500 pans were still being used by the 1960s but nowadays only about 150 are going concerns. The first written reference to the collection of salt in these parts was in AD 822, but it seems pretty likely the Romans had a go too.

During Semana Santa, Salinas comes to life; Judas is put on trial by the villagers. However, it's something of a kangaroo court as he's always convicted and burned.

Cañón de Delika
To get to the car park, which is about 3 km from the main road, the A2625 (running from Orduña in the north to Espejo in the south and beyond to Burgos) turn-off at the signpost for 'Monte Santiago' and is about 8 km south of Orduña.

To the west beyond Salinas, and actually reached via the province of Burgos, is this spectacular canyon that widens into the valley of Orduña (Aiaraldea). The Río Nervión has its source near here and when running (only in the rainy season), it spectacularly spills 270 m into the gorge below: the highest waterfall in Spain. There's a good 90-minute round walk from the car park. Follow the right-hand road first, which brings you to the falls, then follow the cliffs along to the left, where vultures soar above the valley below. When you reach the second mirador, looking down the valley to Orduña, there's another road that descends through beech forest back to the car park. Near the car park is a spring, the **Fuente de Santiago**. Legend has it that St James stopped here to refresh himself and his horse during his alleged time in Spain.

Listings Western Alava

Transport

Salinas de Añana
Bus
5 buses daily from **Vitoria** bus station.

Cañón de Delika
There are buses to Orduña from Vitoria bus station with **La Unión** and trains from Bilbao with **RENFE**.

Eastern Alava

medieval villages at the base of the Pyrenees

The eastern half of the Alava plain is dotted with interesting villages, churches and prehistoric remains. The town of Salvatierra is the most convenient base for exploration or walking. At the northern fringes of the plain, the mountains rise into Guipúzcoa. One of the Camino de Santiago routes passes through the natural tunnel of San Adrián here.

Salvatierra/Agurain

The major centre in eastern Alava is the not-very-major Salvatierra (Agurain), a well-preserved, walled medieval town with some interesting buildings. Around Salvatierra there's plenty of walking, canyoning and abseiling to be done, while further afield canoeing, windsurfing, paragliding and horse trekking can be arranged. The sleeping and eating possibilities are nothing to write home about, but there's a *pensión* and a *casa rural* in town. The tourist office (see Tourist information, page 109), on the main street half a block up from the square with the **Iglesia de San Juan**, is very helpful. They currently hold keys for the churches in Salvatierra as well as the marvellous church at Gaceo. Unfortunately, though, they don't have permission to lend the keys to visitors so currently the only option is to pay for a guided tour. A guided trip to Gaceo and Alaiza costs €5 per person: contact the tourist office or check their website for details. If there's no tour that coincides with your visit, you can organize a private tour for €25.

Gaceo and Alaiza

Worth paying to visit from Salvatierra (see above), the frescoes in **Gaceo**'s small village church, San Martín, are extremely impressive. The 13th-century building's interior is completely covered with the works, dated to the 14th century. They were rediscovered in the 1960s, having been hidden under a healthy coat of plaster. The major scene is a

Trinity above the altar, a Crucifixion, and the Last Judgement, with St Michael carefully weighing souls.

Nearby, in the village of **Alaiza**, the Iglesia de La Asunción is similarly painted, but in a bizarrely different, seemingly irreligious style and a childlike technique. It's far from high medieval art, but the pictures are extremely funny – especially to fans of toilet humour.

Túnel de San Adrián and around

One of the most interesting walks starts from the hamlet of Zalduondo, 8 km north of Salvatierra. A section of the Camino del Norte variant of the **Camino de Santiago**, part of it follows the old Roman/medieval highway that effectively linked most of the peninsula with the rest of Europe. It's about 5.5 km from Zalduondo (up a very poor road) to a small parking area named **Zumarraundi**. From there, the track ascends through beech forest to the Túnel de San Adrián. Shortly after meeting the old stone road, there's a right turn up a slope that's easy to miss; look for the wooden signpost at the top of the rise to your right. The tunnel is a spectacular natural cave cutting a path through the hill. It houses a small chapel, perhaps built to assuage the fears of medieval pilgrims, many of whom thought that the cave was the entrance to Hell. After the tunnel, the trail continues into Guipúzcoa, reaching the attractive town of Zegama about 90 minutes' walk further on. There are numerous adventure tourism options in the area.

Eguilaz

The area around Zalduondo and Salvatierra is also notable for its prehistoric remains; in particular a series of dolmens. Near the village of Eguilaz 45 minutes' walk from Salvatierra (just off the N1 to the east) is the dolmen of **Aitzkomendi**, which was rediscovered by a ploughing farmer in 1830. What happened to the plough is unrecorded, but the 11 impressive stones making up the structure all tip the scales at around the 10-ton mark. It's thought that the dolmen is a funerary marker dating from the early Bronze Age. On weekdays, five buses run to Zalduondo from Vitoria/Salvatierra (destination Araia); two run on Saturday and one on Sunday.

Sorginetxe and around

On the other side of Salvatierra near Arrizala is the equally impressive Sorginetxe, dated to a similar period. The name means 'house of the witch'; in the Middle Ages when the area was still heavily wooded, it could well have been the forest home of somebody of that profession. To the east of here, near the village of Ilarduia, is the **Leze Cave**, a massive crevice in the cliff face. It's 80 m high and a stream flows from its mouth, making access tricky for casual visitors. It's a good place for canyoning (contact the tourist office in Salvatierra, see Tourist information, below).

Gorbeia

North of Vitoria, straddling Vizcaya and Alava, is the massif of Gorbeia, a protected park and an enticing and difficult-to-access area of peaks and gorges topped by the peak of the same name, which hits 1482 m. It features in Basque consciousness as a realm of deities and purity. There are several good marked trails around **Murgia**, including an ascent of the peak itself, which shouldn't be attempted in poor weather.

Tourist information

Salvatierra

Tourist office
*C Mayor 8, T945 302 931, www.
arabakolautada.eus. Sep-Jun Tue-Sun
1000-1400, Jul-Aug daily 1000-1400
and 1600-2000.*

Where to stay

Salvatierra

€€ Eikolara
*Barrio Arbinatea 30, Zalduondo,
T945 304 332, www.eikolara.com.*
An excellent *casa rural*, this great spot is a
characterfully restored old stone house in
the village of Zalduondo, where there are
another 2 *casas rurales*. The rooms (which
vary in price and size) are colourfully and
stylishly decorated, and the owners are
helpful and keep it all super clean and ship
shape. Breakfast included.

€€ Zadorra Etxea
*C Zadorra 21, Salvatierra-Agurain,
T945 312 427, www.zadorraetxea.com.*

Although often let out whole over weekends,
this *casa rural* does offer accommodation
on a per-room basis. Friendly owners and
thoughtful decoration with exposed beams
and wooden floors make this Salvatierra's
best place to stay.

€ Mendiaxpe
*Barrio Salsamendi 22, Araia, T945 304 212,
www.mendiaxpe.com.*
Cleverly located in the wooded foothills of
the Sierra de Urkilla, this is a superb base for
walking in the area. There's use of a kitchen
but no meals available except breakfast. The
3 en suite rooms are lovely and light.

Transport

Salvatierra
Bus
There are **Burundesa** buses hourly from
Vitoria bus station to Salvatierra, 40 mins.

Gorbeia
Bus
There are 4-5 daily buses to Murgia from
Vitoria bus station.

Rioja Alavesa

gorgeous hilltop town in an area known for its vineyards

Basque Rioja? The two words don't seem to go together naturally but in fact many
of the finest Riojas are from Alava province. Confusion reigns because the Spanish
province of La Rioja is only one of three that the wine region of the same name
encompasses. Although it's not far from Vitoria, the Rioja Alavesa definitely feels
Spanish rather than Basque; the descent from the green hills into the arid plains
crosses a cultural and geographical border. As well as the opportunity to visit some
excellent wineries – and there are nearly 400 in the region – the hilltop town of
Laguardia is one of the most atmospheric places in Northern Spain.

★ Laguardia

The small, walled hilltop town of Laguardia (Biasteri in Euskara) commands the plain
like a sentinel – which it was; it was originally called La Guardia de Navarra (the guard of
Navarra). Underneath the medieval streets, like catacombs, are some 230 small bodegas,

cellars used for the making and storing of wine, as well as a place to hide in troubled times. Most are no longer used – **Bodega El Fabulista** is a fascinating exception.

Even if wine is put aside for a moment, the town itself is captivating. Founded in 1164, its narrow streets are a lovely place to wander. Traffic is almost prohibited due to the bodegas carved out 6 m below. The impressive **Iglesia de Santa María de los Reyes** ① *tours daily Mon-Sat, €2, reserve at tourist office*, begun in the 12th century, has an extraordinarily well-preserved painted Gothic façade, while the former Ayuntamiento on the arched Plaza Nueva was inaugurated in the 16th century under Carlos V. Other visitable attractions include the fortress-church of San Juan and a cistern dating back to Celtiberian times.

Laguardia was the birthplace of the 18th-century fable writer Félix de Samaniego.

Around Laguardia

The area around Laguardia also has a few non-vinous attractions. A set of small lakes close by is one of Spain's better spots for birdwatching, particularly from September to March when migrating birds are around. There are a series of marked walking and cycling routes in this area, spectacularly backed by the mountains of the Sierra Cantábrica.

If you're coming from Vitoria by car, it's marginally quicker and much more scenic to take the smaller A2124 rather than the motorway. After ascending to a pass, the high ground dramatically drops away to the Riojan plain; there's a superb lookout on the road, justly known as 'El Balcón' (the balcony). From here, the whole of the Rioja region is visible before and below you.

Wineries

Bodegas Palacio ① *Ctra de Elciego s/n, T945 600 057, www.bodegaspalacio.com, phone for times, visits €15-25; booking essential.* One of the handiest of the wineries, and worth seeing, is Bodegas Palacio, located just below Laguardia on

> **Tip...**
> The website www.rutadelvinoderioja alavesa.com gives details of all the area's wineries and visiting times.

the Elciego road, some 10 minutes' walk from town. Palacio produces a range of wines, the quality of which has increased in recent years. Their Glorioso and Cosme Palacio labels are widely sold in the UK.

The winery was originally founded in 1894 and is fairly typical of the area, producing 90% red wine from the Tempranillo grape, and a small 10% of white from Viura (as well as *crianzas, reservas* and *gran reservas*). Palacio also produce a red wine for drinking young, Milflores, which is soft, fruity and a change from the woodier Rioja styles. At time of research, there were extensive changes being made to the winery, including new visitor experiences, so call ahead to see what's available.

Bodega El Fabulista ① *Plaza San Juan s/n, Laguardia, T945 621 192, www.bodega elfabulista.com. Tours daily at 1130, 1300, 1730, and 1900; Sun: mornings only, €7.* A massive contrast to Palacio, which produces two million bottles a year, is Bodega El Fabulista, within the walls of Laguardia. The wine is made using very traditional methods in the intriguing underground cellar. The wines, marketed as Decidido, are a good young-drinking red and white. The tours are excellent and atmospheric and include lots of background information on the Rioja wine region and a generous tasting in a beautiful underground vault.

Herederos del Marqués de Riscal ⓘ *C Torrea 1, Elciego, T945 180 888, www.marques deriscal.com, multilingual tours Tue-Sat 1000, 1230, 1600, Sun 1100 and 1300, €12, reserve in advance; you can book and pay online.* Founded in 1860, Marqués de Riscal is the oldest and best known of the Rioja bodegas and has built a formidable reputation for the quality of its wines. The Marqués himself was a Madrid journalist who, having cooled off in France after getting in some hot political water at home, returned to Spain and started making wine. Enlisting the help of Monsieur Pinot, a French expert, he experimented by planting Cabernet Sauvignon, which is still used in the wines today.

The innovative spirit continues, and Marqués de Riscal enlisted none other than Frank Gehry of Guggenheim museum fame to design their visitor complex, a visual treat of a building. Gehry's design incorporates ribbons of coloured titanium over a building of natural stone. The silver, gold and 'dusty rose' sheets are Gehry's response to 'the unbroken landscape of vineyards and rich tones'. The building encompasses a hotel, a restaurant, and an oenotherapy spa, which combines water treatments with applications of grape and vine extracts.

The winery is modern but remains faithful to the bodega's rigorous tradition of quality. As well as their traditionally elegant Reserva and Gran Reserva, the more recently inaugurated Barón de Chirel is a very classy red indeed, coming from low-yielding old vines and exhibiting a more French character than is typical of the region.

Other wineries Two kilometres north of Laguardia, with a waved design echoing the steep mountains behind it, is **Ysios Bodega** ⓘ *T945 600 640, www.ysios.com, visits are daily at 1100 and 1300, plus 1600 Mon-Fri, €12, they need to be pre-arranged*, designed by Santiago Calatrava, the brilliant Valencian engineer/architect who has contributed so much to Euskadi.

Twenty minutes east of Laguardia is the pretty but parched town of Oyón/Oion. One of the bigger operations here is **Bodegas Faustino Martínez** ⓘ *T945 622 500, www. bodegasfaustino.com, tours weekdays during working hours and Sat 1030-1300, phone to arrange, €7*, whose range of Faustino wines are a reliable and popular choice both in Spain and the UK. They run a good tour of their operation in Spanish or English. The tour is all the better for being a bit more in-depth and a little less cursory than some of the other big wineries.

Though not strictly a winery, **Centro Temático Villa Lucía** ⓘ *Ctra Logroño s/n, T945 600 032, www.villa-lucia.com, Tue-Sat 1000-1400, 1700-2000, Sun 1000-1400, book in advance, €6.50*, is definitely a winey experience. It offers a 4D presentation and intriguing 'virtual' tasting sessions that'll help hone your skills, and you can also pre-arrange a variety of different tasting sessions of the real stuff. There's also a botanic garden here and a good restaurant.

Tourist information

Laguardia

Tourist office
C Mayor 52, T945 600 845, www.laguardia-
alava.com. Mon-Fri 1000-1400 and 1600-
1900, Sat 1000-1400 and 1700-1900, Sun
1045-1400.

Where to stay

There are some excellent places to stay in
Laguardia and an ever-mushrooming crop
of design hotels in the surrounding area.

Laguardia

€€€ Castillo El Collado
Paseo El Collado 1, T945 621 200,
www.hotelcollado.com.
Decorated in plush but colourful style, this
mansion at the north end of the old town is
comfortable and welcoming. There are 10
individually decorated rooms as well as a
restaurant. The owner is more than helpful,
and can arrange your bodega visits for you.
Recommended.

€€€ Hospedería de los Parajes
C Mayor 46, T945 621 130, www.
hospederiadelosparajes.com.
Right in the heart of the old town, this hotel
offers significant style and comfort and
peaceful rooms with excellent facilities.
There's a range of room classes at different
prices and sizes, but all boast chic fabrics and
modern-rustic design and great bathrooms.
There's a wonderful underground bodega
that makes a romantic spot for an evening
glass of local wine. Recommended.

€€€ Posada Mayor de Migueloa
C Mayor 20, T945 600 187,
www.mayordemigueloa.com.
A beautifully decorated Spanish country
house, with lovely old wooden furniture
and a peaceful atmosphere. Rooms are

heated and a/c. The restaurant is of a similarly
high standard.

€ Larretxori
Portal de Páganos s/n, T945 600 763,
www.nekatur.net/larretxori.
This comfortable agroturismo is just outside
the city walls and commands excellent
views over the area. The rooms are spruce,
clean and good value and the owner is
very benevolent.

Around Laguardia

€€€€ Eguren Ugarte
A124, Km 61, Páganos, T945 600 766,
www.egurenugarte.com.
Topped by an outrageous turret visible for
miles around, this boutique wine hotel offers
wonderful views of the region. Rooms are
spacious, comfortable and very peaceful
and there's an excellent restaurant featuring
the property's wines, which are made in the
subterranean bodega underneath you.

€€€€ Hotel Marqués de Riscal
T945 180 880, C Torrea 1, Elciego,
www.hotel-marquesderiscal.com.
This flamboyant structure is visible from
afar and is your chance to stay in a Frank
Gehry-designed building. The exuberant
waves of metal conceal a modern building
made from traditional stone. The rooms are,
as you'd expect at this price, well designed if
not enormous, and have appealingly offbeat
shapes and features. You'll get better rates
from the website the further in advance you
book. There's also a fine gourmet restaurant.

€€€€ Hotel Viura
C Mayor s/n, Villabuena de Alava,
T945 609 000, www.hotelviura.com.
Blending exuberant contemporary
architecture and elegant interior design,
this striking place is in a winemaking village
10 km west of Laguardia and makes a top
base for wine touring. While the exterior

is a lighthearted riot of cubes and angles, the rooms are sleek and spacious, and the helpful crew that run it will bend over backwards to make your stay a pleasant one. There's a good restaurant and great facilities – the only thing missing is a pool, though the municipal one is adjacent.

Restaurants

Laguardia

€€ Amelibia
C Barbacana 14, T945 621 207, www.restauranteamelibia.com. Lunchtimes Wed-Mon and evenings Fri and Sat only.
Offering a lovely view over vineyards, this is a warmly welcoming restaurant that has stylish cuisine based on excellent local produce and traditions but with plenty of contemporary flair and innovative flavour combinations. Hearty meat and game dishes and deli-style appetizers form the core of the menu.

€€ Castillo El Collado
Paseo El Collado 1, T945 621 200, www.hotelcollado.com.
There's an excellent, well-priced restaurant with 3 attractive eating areas in this beautiful fortified hotel at the northern end of Laguardia.

€€ El Bodegón
Travesía Santa Engracia 3, T945 600 793.
Tucked away in the middle of old Laguardia is this cosy restaurant, with a *menú del día*

focusing on the hearty staples of the region, such as *pochas* (beans) or *patatas con chorizo*.

€ Bar Hiruko
C Santa Engracia 42, T945 600 644, www.hirukolaguardia.com.
Quite a contrast to this medieval town, this modern bar-café is nevertheless Laguardia's best option for *pintxos*, which are elaborate and innovative. It also does a range of good-value *raciones*. Nearby **Berria Taberna** at number 28 is another excellent *pintxo* option.

Bars and clubs

Laguardia

Café Tertulia
C Mayor 70, www.bartertulialaguardia.com.
With couches, padded booths and a pool table, this is the best place for a few quiet drinks in Laguardia.

Transport

Laguardia
Bus
There are a few daily buses to Laguardia from **Vitoria** (1 hr), **Logroño** (15-25 mins) and **Haro** (40 mins). There is 1 bus each way between **Bilbao** to Laguardia and 1 Mon-Fri to **Elciego**.

Around Laguardia
Bus
Elciego is served several times daily from **Logroño** (35 mins).

Practicalities

Getting there

Air

Flights from the UK

The cheapest direct flights are with the budget operators, whose fares can be as low as €30 return but are more usually €80-200. It's easier to get hold of a cheaper fare if you fly off-season or midweek, and if you book well in advance. Bilbao is the Basque Country's main airport, and there are direct flights there from Britain. **Easyjet** serves Bilbao from London, as do **British Airways**, while **Ryanair** fly to Santander with connecting bus service to Bilbao, not much more than an hour away. **Easyjet** also have a direct service from Manchester and Bristol. **Ryanair** and **Easyjet** also fly to Biarritz, France, which is 30 minutes on the train to the Spanish border, from where it's another 30 minutes to San Sebastián. These budget routes are subject to frequent change.

You may also find that it's cheaper to connect via Madrid or Barcelona. **Vueling**, **Ryanair** and **Iberia** have useful domestic Spanish networks that include Bilbao.

From Madrid airport (Barajas), it's very easy to hop in a taxi or the metro to the bus station (metro stop: Méndez Alvaro) or train station (Chamartín) and be in Northern Spain in a jiffy. Before booking, it's worth doing a bit of online research. A good site for flight comparisons is www.kayak.com, which compares prices from travel agencies and websites. **Flightmapper** ① *www.flightmapper.net*, is great for finding the most convenient routes between you and your destination. **Flightchecker** ① *http://flightchecker.moneysavingexpert.com*, is handy for checking multiple dates for budget airline deals. Another useful tool for its flexibility is at http://matrix.itasoftware.com, and www.opodo.com has up-to-date prices from a large confederation of airlines.

Flights from Europe

There are several direct flights from a range of European destinations, including Dublin, to Bilbao. There are flights to Madrid and Barcelona from most European capitals with both budget and full-fare carriers.

Rail

Travelling from the UK to Northern Spain by train is unlikely to save either time or money; the only advantages lie in the pleasure of the journey itself, the chance to stop along the way, and the environmental impact of flying versus rail travel. Using **Eurostar** ① *T0870 160 6600, www.eurostar.com*, changing stations in Paris and boarding a TGV to Hendaye can have you in San Sebastián 10 hours after leaving St Pancras if the connections are kind. Once across the Channel, the trains are reasonably priced, but factor in £100-400 return on **Eurostar** and things don't look so rosy, unless you can take advantage of a special offer. Using the train/Channel ferry combination will more or less halve the cost and double the time.

Trains to Hendaye leave from Gare Montparnasse, though these may return to the Gare Austerlitz when that station's refurbishment is concluded.

If you are planning the train journey, **Rail Europe** ① *T0844 484 064, www.raileurope.co.uk*, is a useful company. **RENFE**, Spain's rail network, has online timetables at www.renfe.es. Also see the extremely useful www.seat61.com.

Road

Bus

Eurolines ⓘ *www.eurolines.com*, run several buses from major European cities to a variety of destinations in Northern Spain; there are several morning buses a week, that pull into Bilbao some 21 hours later after a change in Paris. There's an extra bus in summer. A return fare costs about £180; it's marginally cheaper for pensioners and students, but overall isn't great value unless you're not a fan of flying.

Car

The main route into the Basque Country is the E05/E70 motorway that runs down the southwest coast of France, crossing into Spain at Irún, near San Sebastián. This motorway is tolled but worthwhile compared to the slow, traffic-plagued *rutas nacionales*.

Cars must be insured for third party and practically any driving licence is acceptable (but if you're from a country that a Guardia Civil would struggle to locate on a map, take an International Driving Licence).

Sea

Bear in mind that from the UK it's usually cheaper to fly and hire a car in Northern Spain than bring the motor across on the ferry. For competitive fares by sea to France and Spain, check with **Ferrysavers** ⓘ *T0844 576 8835, www.ferrysavers.com*, **Direct Ferries** ⓘ *www.directferries.co.uk*, and **www.ferrycheap.com**, which list special offers from various operators. The website **www.seat61.com** is good for investigating train/ferry combinations.

The handiest service is run by **Brittany Ferries** ⓘ *T0871 244 0744, www.brittany-ferries.co.uk*, from Portsmouth to Bilbao. There are twice-weekly sailings on each route, taking around 24 hours. Prices are variable but can usually be found for about £70-90 each way in a reclining seat. A car adds about £150 each way, and cabins start from about £80.

The same company also run ferries from Plymouth and Portsmouth to Santander, just over an hour's drive from Bilbao.

Getting around

Public transport in the Basque Country is excellent, with a comprehensive, fast bus service between cities and towns, and a good network of local and long-distance trains.

Rail

The Spanish national rail network **RENFE** ⓘ *T902 240 202 (English-speaking operators), www.renfe.com*, connects the major Basque cities with each other and with Madrid, among other places.

Prices vary significantly according to the type of service you are using. The standard fast-ish intercity service is called **Alvia**. Slower local trains are called *regionales*.

It's always worth buying a ticket in advance for long-distance travel, as trains are often full. The best option is to buy them via the website, which sometimes offers advance-purchase discounts. They'll send a ticket to your email or mobile; you can also print off tickets at the station using the reservation code. You can also book by phone, but they only accept Spanish debit and credit cards. If buying your ticket at the station, allow plenty of time for queuing. Ticket windows are labelled *venta anticipada* (in advance) and *venta inmediata* (six hours or less before the journey).

All Spanish trains are non-smoking. The faster trains have first-class (*preferente*) and second-class sections as well as a *cafetería*. First class costs about 30% more than standard and can be a worthwhile deal.

An **ISIC student card** or **under-26 card** grants a discount of 20% to 30% on train services. If you're using a European railpass, be aware that you'll still have to make a reservation on Spanish trains and pay the small reservation fee (which covers your insurance).

There are two other networks in the Basque Country. First is **FEVE** ⓘ *www.renfe.com (now operated by RENFE but listed as a separate service)*, whose main line runs along the north coast from Bilbao to Santander, Asturias, and as far as Ferrol in Galicia; there's another line from Bilbao to León. It's a slow line, but very picturesque. It stops at many small villages and is handy for exploring the coast. The other is **Eusko Trenbideak** ⓘ *www. euskotren.es*, a short-haul train service with good coverage of the coast and inland towns.

Both **FEVE** and **RENFE** operate short-distance *cercanías* (commuter trains), essentially suburban train services. These are particularly helpful around Bilbao.

Road

Bus

Buses have traditionally been the staple of Spanish public transport. Services between Basque towns and cities are fast, frequent, reliable and cheap; the five-hour trip from Madrid to Oviedo, for example, costs €34. When buying a ticket, always check how long the journey will take, as the odd bus will be an 'all stations to' job, calling in at villages that seem surprised to even see it. *Directo* is the term for a bus that doesn't stop; it won't usually cost any more either. Various premium services (called *Supra*, *Ejecutivo* or similar) add comfort, with onboard drinks service, lounge area in the bus station and more space, but cost around 60% more.

Most places have a single terminal, the *estación de autobuses*, which is where all short- and long-haul services leave from. Buy your tickets at the relevant window; if there isn't one, buy it from the driver. Most tickets will have a seat number (*asiento*) on them; ask when buying the ticket if you prefer a window (*ventana*) or aisle (*pasillo*) seat. There's a huge number of bus companies, some of which allow phone and online booking; the most useful in the Basque Country are **Bizkaibus** ① *www.bizkaia.net*, **Pesa** ① *www.pesa. net*, and **ALSA** ① *T902 422 242, www.alsa.e*s. The platform that the bus leaves from is called a *dársena* or *andén*. If you're travelling at busy times (particularly a fiesta or national holiday) always book the bus ticket in advance.

The Basque cities are fairly compact, and Bilbao has metro and tram services, so you won't find local buses particularly necessary. There's a fairly comprehensive network in most towns, though; the Transport sections in this guide indicate where they come in handy. In most cities, you just board and pay the driver.

Car

The roads in the Basque Country are good, excellent in many parts. While driving isn't as sedate as in parts of Northern Europe, it's generally of a very high standard, and you'll have few problems. To drive in Spain, you'll need a full driving licence from your home country. This applies to virtually all foreign nationals, but in practice, if you're from an 'unusual' country, consider an International Driving Licence or official translation of your licence into Spanish.

There are two types of motorway, *autovías* and *autopistas*; the quality of both is generally excellent, with a speed limit of 120 kph. They are signposted in blue and may have tolls payable, in which case there'll be a red warning circle on the blue sign when you're entering the motorway. An 'A' prefix to the road number indicates a motorway; an 'AP' prefix indicates a toll motorway. Tolls are expensive in the Basque Country. You can pay by cash or card.

Rutas nacionales form the backbone of Spain's road network. Centrally administered, they vary wildly in quality. Typically, they are choked with traffic backed up behind trucks, and there are few stretches of dual carriageway. Driving at siesta time is a good idea if you're going to be on a busy stretch. *Rutas nacionales* are marked with a red 'N' number. The speed limit now varies between 70 and 90 kph outside built-up areas, as it does for secondary roads, which are numbered with a provincial prefix.

In urban areas, the speed limit varies between 30 and 50 kph. Many towns and villages have sensors that will turn traffic lights red if you're over the limit on approach. City driving can be confusing, with signposting generally poor and traffic heavy; it's worth carrying a GPS or printing off the directions that your hotel may send you with a reservation. In some towns and cities, many of the hotels are officially signposted, making things easier. Larger cities may have their historic quarter blocked off by barriers: if your hotel lies within these, ring the buzzer and say the name of the hotel, and the barriers will open.

Police are increasingly enforcing speed limits in Spain, and foreign drivers are liable to a large on-the-spot fine. Drivers can also be punished for not carrying two red warning triangles to place on the road in case of breakdown, a bulb-replacement kit and a fluorescent green waistcoat to wear if you break down by the side of the road. Drink driving is being cracked down on more than was once the case; the limit is 0.5 g/l of blood, slightly lower than the equivalent in England, for example.

Parking is a problem in nearly every town and city in Northern Spain. Red or yellow lines on the side of the street mean no parking. Blue lines indicate a metered zone, while white lines mean that some restriction is in place; a sign will give details. Parking meters can usually only be dosed up for a maximum of two hours, but they take a siesta at lunchtime too. Print the ticket off and display it in the car. Once the day's period has expired, you can charge it up for the next morning to avoid an early start. If you get a ticket, you can pay a minimal fine at the machine within the first half hour or hour instead of the full whack (though it must be said that parking fines are rarely even pursued outside the city they are issued in, let alone in another country). Underground car parks are common and well signposted, but fairly pricey; €15-25 a day is normal. However, this is the safest option if you are going to leave any valuables in your car. Hotels without private parking may offer a special deal with a nearby underground car park – find out before you park as once you've taken the ticket it may be too late. A useful website is **www.parkopedia.com**, which will enable you to find the cheapest parking around town.

Liability insurance is required for every car driven in Spain and you must carry proof of it. If bringing your own car, check carefully with your insurers that you're covered, and get a certificate (green card). If your insurer doesn't cover you for breakdowns, consider joining the **RACE** ⓘ *T900 100 992, www.race.es*, Spain's automobile association, which provides good breakdown cover.

Hiring a car in Spain is easy. The major multinationals have offices at all large towns and airports; the company with the broadest network is **National/ATESA** ⓘ *www.atesa.es*. Brokers, such as www.autoeurope.com and www.webcarhire.com, are usually cheaper than booking direct with the rental companies. Prices start at around €100 per week for a small car with unlimited mileage. You'll need a credit card and most agencies will either not accept under 25s or demand a surcharge. Rates from the airports tend to be cheaper than from towns. Before booking, use a price-comparison website like www.kayak.com to find the best deals.

Cycling

Basques are crazy for competitive cycling and though this doesn't translate into loving it as a means of transport, the region's cities are among Spain's best for getting around by bike, with reasonable bike lane coverage and plenty of hire options.

Motorcycling

Motorcycling is a good way to enjoy the Basque Country and there are few difficulties to trouble the biker; bike shops and mechanics are relatively common. Hiring a motorbike is possible in Bilbao.

Taxis

Taxis are a good option; flagfall is €2-4 in most places (it increases slightly at night and on Sundays). A taxi is available if its green light is lit; hail one on the street or ask for the nearest rank (*parada de taxis*). In smaller towns or at quiet times, you'll have to ring for one. All towns have their own taxi company; phone numbers are given in the text.

Maps

While online mapping is the way many go now, if you want a paper version, Michelin road maps are reliable for general navigation. If you're getting off the beaten track you'll often find a local map handy. Tourist offices provide these, which vary in quality. The best topographical maps are published by the **Instituto Geográfico Nacional** (IGN). These are not necessarily more accurate than those obtainable in Britain or North America. A useful website for route planning is www.guiarepsol.com. Car hire companies have navigation systems available, though they cost a hefty supplement; you're better off bringing your own.

Stanfords ⓘ *12-14 Long Acre, Covent Garden, London WC2E 9LP, T020 7836 1321, www.stanfords.co.uk*, with well-travelled staff and 40,000 titles in stock, is the world's largest map and travel bookshop. It also has a branch at 29 Corn Street, Bristol.

Essentials A-Z

Accident and emergency

There are various emergency numbers, but the general one across the nation is T112. This will get you the police, ambulance, or fire brigade. T091 gets just the police.

Children

Kids are kings in Spain, and it's one of the easiest places to take them along on holiday. Children socialize with their parents from an early age here, and you'll see them eating in restaurants and out in bars well after midnight. The outdoor summer life and high pedestrianization of the cities is especially suitable and stress-free for both you and the kids to enjoy the experience.

Spaniards are friendly and accommodating towards children, and you'll undoubtedly get treated better with them than without. Few places, however, are equipped with highchairs, unbreakable plates or baby-changing facilities. Children are expected to eat the same food as their parents, although you'll sometimes see a *menú infantil* at a restaurant, which typically has simpler dishes and smaller portions.

The cut-off age for children paying half or no admission/passage on public transport and in tourist attractions varies widely. **RENFE** trains let children under 4 travel for free, and its discount passage of around 50% applies up to the age of 12. Most car rental companies have child seats available, but it's wise to book these in advance.

As for attractions, beaches are an obvious highlight, but many of the newer museums are hands-on, and playgrounds and parks are common. Campsites cater to families and the larger ones often have child-minding facilities and activities.

Customs and duty free

Non-EU citizens are allowed to import 1 litre of spirits, 2 litres of wine and 200 cigarettes or 250 g of tobacco or 50 cigars. EU citizens are theoretically limited by personal use only.

Electricity

Spain uses the standard European 230V plug, with 2 round pins.

Health

Health for travellers in Spain is rarely a problem. Medical facilities are good, and the worst most travellers experience is an upset stomach, usually merely a result of the different diet rather than any bug.

The water is safe to drink. The sun in Spain can be harsh, so take adequate precautions to prevent heat exhaustion/sunburn. Many medications that require a prescription in other countries are available over the counter at pharmacies in Spain. Pharmacists are highly trained but don't necessarily speak English. In all medium-sized towns and cities, at least one pharmacy is open 24 hrs; this is organized on a rota system, with details posted in the window of all pharmacies and in local newspapers. Ask your hotel to recommend a hospital or English-speaking doctor should you need one.

Medical services

Hospital de Basurto, Av Montevideo 18, Bilbao, T944 006 000, T944 755 000, Tram Basurto.

Hospital Nuestra Señora de Arantzazu, Av Doctor Begiristain 115, San Sebastián, T943 007 000.

Insurance

European Union citizens should get hold of a **European Health Insurance Card** (**EHIC**), available for now via www.dh.gov.uk or from post offices in the UK, before leaving home. This guarantees free medical care throughout the EU. Other citizens should seriously consider medical insurance, but check for reciprocal Spanish cover with your private or public health scheme first.

Insurance is a good idea anyway to cover you for theft, etc. In the event of theft, you'll have to make a report at the local police station within 24 hrs and obtain a report to show your insurers. (English levels at the police station are likely to be low, so try to take a Spanish speaker with you to help.)

Internet

Internet cafés have effectively disappeared, and most travellers will access the internet via Wi-Fi or mobile data. Just about all accommodation has free Wi-Fi, as do many cafés. If you've got an unlocked phone, it's easy to buy a pay-as-you-go Spanish SIM card with a data package. Roaming costs within the EU have been abolished, so EU citizens can use their home mobile without incurring extra charges. It remains to be seen whether the UK will continue to be part of this.

Language

For travelling purposes, everyone in the Basque Country speaks Spanish, known either as Castellano or Español, and it's a huge help to know some. Most young people know some English, and standards are rapidly rising, but don't assume that people aged 40 or over know any at all. Spaniards are often shy to attempt to speak English. While many visitor attractions have some sort of information available in English (and to a lesser extent French and German), many don't, or have English tours only in times of high demand. Most tourist office staff will speak at least some English, and there's a good range of translated information available in most places. See the What to do sections in listings for details of language schools.

While efforts to speak the language are appreciated, it's more or less expected, to the same degree as English is expected in Britain or the USA. Nobody will be rude if you don't speak any Spanish, but nobody will think to slow their rapidfire stream of the language for your benefit either, or pat you on the back for producing a few phrases in their tongue.

The other language you'll come across is Euskara/Euskera (the Basque language). Euskara is wholly unrelated to Spanish; if you're interested in Basque culture, by all means learn a few words (and make instant friends), but be aware that many people in Euskadi aren't Basque, and that it's quite a political issue.

Money *Check www.xe.com for exchange rates.*

Currency

In 2002, Spain switched to the euro, bidding farewell to the peseta. The euro (€) is divided into 100 *céntimos*. Euro notes are standard across the whole eurozone, and come in denominations of 5, 10, 20, 50, 100, and the rarely seen 200 and 500. Coins have one standard face and one national face; all coins are, however, acceptable in all countries. The coins are slightly difficult to tell apart when you're not used to them. The coppers are 1, 2 and 5 cent pieces, the golds are 10, 20 and 50, and the silver/gold combinations are €1 and €2. People still tend to think in pesetas when talking about large amounts like house prices.

ATMs and banks

The best way to get money in Spain is by plastic. ATMs are plentiful in Spain, and accept all the major international debit and credit cards. The Spanish bank won't charge for the transaction, though they will charge a mark-up on the exchange rate, but beware of your own bank hitting you for a hefty fee: check with them before leaving home. Even if they do, it's likely to be a better deal than exchanging cash. The website www.moneysavingexpert.com has a good rundown on the most economical ways of accessing cash while travelling, including prepaid cards.

Banks are usually open 0830-1400 Mon-Fri (and sometimes Sat in winter) and many change foreign money (sometimes only the central branch in a town will do it). Commission rates vary widely; it's usually best to change large amounts, as there's often a minimum commission of €6 or so. Nevertheless, banks nearly always give better rates than change offices (*casas de cambio*), which are fewer by the day. If you're stuck outside banking hours, some large department stores such as the Corte Inglés change money at knavish rates. Traveller's cheques are still accepted in here and there, but have basically gone the way of the dodo.

Tax
Nearly all goods and services in Spain are subject to a value-added tax (IVA). This is only 10% for most things the traveller will encounter, including food and hotels, and 4% for basics like vegetables and books but is 21% on other consumer goods. IVA is normally included in the stated prices. You're technically entitled to claim it back if you're a non-EU citizen, for purchases over €90. If you're buying something pricey, make sure you get a tax receipt (*factura*) clearly showing the IVA component, as well as your name and passport number; you can claim the amount back at major airports on departure. Some shops will have a form to smooth the process.

Cost of living and travelling
Though far from a budget destination these days, Spain can still be a reasonably cheap place to travel if you're prepared to forgo a few luxuries. If you're travelling as a pair, staying in cheap *pensiones*, eating a set meal at lunchtime, travelling short distances by bus or train daily, and snacking on *pintxos* in the evenings, €65 per person per day is reasonable. If you camp and grab picnic lunches from shops, you could reduce this considerably. In a cheap hotel or good *hostal* and using a car, €130 each a day and you'll not be counting pennies; €250 per day and you'll be very comfy indeed unless you're staying in 4- or 5-star accommodation.

Accommodation is more expensive in summer than in winter, particularly on the coast. San Sebastián is expensive in general, particularly for sleeping, eating and drinking. The news isn't great for the solo traveller; single rooms tend not to be particularly good value, and they are in short supply. Prices range from 60% to 80% of the double/twin price; some establishments even charge the full rate. If you're going to be staying in 3- to 5-star hotels, booking them ahead online can save a lot of money.

Public transport is generally cheap; intercity bus services are quick and low-priced and trains are reasonable, though the fast AVE trains cost substantially more.

Standard unleaded petrol has varied in recent years from €1 to €1.50 per litre. Diesel is about €0.10 cheaper. In some places, particularly in tourist areas, you may be charged up to 20% more to sit outside a restaurant. It's also worth checking if the 10% IVA (sales tax) is included in menu prices, especially in the more expensive restaurants; it should say on the menu whether this is the case.

Post
The Spanish post is notoriously inefficient and slow by European standards. Post offices (*correos*) generally open Mon-Fri 0800-1300, 1700-2000; Sat 0800-1300, although main offices in large towns stay open all day. Stamps can be bought here or at tobacconists (*estancos*).

Safety

While Bilbao has a few dodgy areas, the Basque Country is a very safe destination. Tourist crime is very low in this region, and you're more likely to have something returned (that you left on that train) than something stolen. That said, don't invite crime by leaving luggage or cash in cars. If parking in a city or, particularly, a popular hiking zone, try to make it clear there's nothing to nick inside by opening the glovebox, etc.

There are several types of police, helpful enough in normal circumstances. The main Basque force is the **Ertzaintza**, the peninsula's most dashing, with cocky red berets. They deal with the day-to-day beat and some crime. The presence of the paramilitary Guardia Civil and Policía Nacional is reduced in Euskadi due to political sensitivity, but they are still present. These **Policía Nacional** are responsible for most urban crimefighting and are the ones to go to if you need to report anything stolen, etc. The **Policía Local/Municipal** are present in large towns and cities and are responsible for some urban crime, as well as traffic control and parking.

Telephone *Country code +34.*

Public phones are fast disappearing, but you'll still see a few around. They accept coins and phone cards, which can be bought from *estancos*.

Domestic landlines have 9-digit numbers beginning with 9 (occasionally with 8). Although the first 3 digits indicate the province, you have to dial the full number from wherever you are calling, including abroad. Mobile numbers start with 6. To dial out of Spain, it's 00 followed by the country code.

Mobile coverage is very good. Most foreign mobiles will work in Spain (although older North American ones won't); check with your service provider about what the call costs will be like. Many mobile networks require you to call up before leaving your home country to activate overseas service ('roaming'). Roaming costs within the European Union have now been eliminated. If you're staying a while, it may be cheaper to buy a Spanish mobile or SIM card, as there are always numerous offers and discounts.

Time

Spain operates on Western European time, ie GMT +1, and changes its clocks in line with the rest of the EU.

'Spanish time' isn't as elastic as it used to be, but if you're told something will happen *'enseguida'* ('straight away') it may take 10 mins, if you're told *'cinco minutos'* (5 mins), grab a seat and a book. Transport leaves promptly.

Tipping

Tipping in Spain is far from compulsory, but much practised. Around 10% is considered extremely generous in a restaurant; 3-5% is more usual. It's rare for a service charge to be added to a bill. Waiters do not normally expect tips but people will often leave something, especially for table service. Taxi drivers don't expect a tip, but will be pleased to receive one.

Tourist information

The Basque tourist information infrastructure is organized by the regional government and is excellent, with a wide range of information, often in English, German and French as well as Euskara and Spanish. Offices within the region can provide maps of the area and towns, and lists of registered accommodation, with 1 booklet for hotels, *hostales* and *pensiones*; another for campsites and another, especially worth picking up, listing farmstay, self-catering and rural accommodation. Opening hours are longer in major cities; many rural offices are only open in summer. Average opening hours are Mon-Sat 1000-1400, 1600-1900, Sun

1000-1400. Offices are often closed on Sun or Mon. Staff often speak English and other European languages and are well trained. The offices (*oficinas de turismo*) are often signposted to some degree within the town or city. Staff may ask where you are from; this is not nosiness but for statistical purposes.

The Basque Country's excellent tourism website is www.turismo.euskadi.eus.

Other useful websites

www.aemet.es Site of the national meteorological institute, with the day's weather and next-day forecasts.

www.airbnb.com Anything in accommodation from a room in somebody's flat to luxurious self-catering houses.

www.alsa.es Northern Spain's major bus operator. Book online.

www.bilbao.net The city's excellent website.

www.blablacar.com Ride-sharing website that's well used in Spain.

www.dgt.es The transport department website has up-to-date information in Spanish on road conditions throughout the country.

www.elpais.com Online edition of Spain's biggest-selling non-sports daily paper. English edition available.

www.euskadi-basquecountry.org Useful source of tourist information, with downloadable content and smartphone apps.

www.guiarepsol.com Excellent online route planner for Spanish roads, also available in English.

www.nekatur.net Extensive listing of farm-stays and *casas rurales* in the Basque region.

www.paginasamarillas.es Yellow Pages.

www.paginasblancas.es The White Pages.

www.parador.es Parador information, including locations, prices and photos.

www.parkopedia.com Great for comparing rates of underground car parks in cities.

www.renfe.com Online timetables and tickets for RENFE train network.

www.soccer-spain.com A website in English dedicated to Spanish football.

www.spain.info The official website of the Spanish tourist board.

www.ticketmaster.es Spain's biggest ticketing agency for concerts, etc, with online purchase.

www.todoturismorural.com, **www.toprural.com** and **www.escapadarural.com** Several of many sites for *casas rurales*.

www.tourspain.es A useful website run by the Spanish tourist board.

Visas

Entry requirements are subject to change, so always check with the Spanish tourist board or an embassy/consulate if you're not an EU citizen. EU citizens and those from countries within the Schengen agreement can enter Spain freely. UK/Irish citizens will need to carry a passport, while an identity card suffices for other EU/Schengen nationals. Citizens of Australia, the USA, Canada, New Zealand, several Latin American countries and Israel can enter without a visa for up to 90 days. Other citizens will require a visa, obtainable from Spanish consulates or embassies. These are usually issued very quickly and valid for all Schengen countries. The basic visa is valid for 90 days, and you'll need 2 passport photos, proof of funds covering your stay and possibly evidence of medical cover (ie insurance). For extensions of visas, apply to an *oficina de extranjeros* in a major city.

Index

Entries in bold refer to maps

FOOTPRINT
Features

Credits

Footprint credits

Editor: Jo Williams
Production and layout: Emma Bryers
Maps: Kevin Feeney
Colour section: Patrick Dawson

Publisher: Felicity Laughton
Patrick Dawson
Marketing: Kirsty Holmes
Sales: Diane McEntee
Advertising and content partnerships:
Debbie Wylde

Photography credits

Front cover: Annavee/Shutterstock.com
Back cover top: Alberto Loyo/
Shutterstock.com
Back cover bottom: Delpixel/
Shutterstock.com
Inside front cover: dvoevnore/Shutterstock.
com, Noradoa/Shutterstock.com.

Colour section
Page 1: Alberto Loyo/Shutterstock.com.
Page 2: Alberto Loyo/Shutterstock.com.
Page 4: Mimadeo/Shutterstock.com.
Page 5: Mariia Levochkina/Shutterstock.
com, Pocholo Calapre/Shutterstock.com,
Lukasz Janyst/Shutterstock.com.
Page 6: Matyas Rehak/Shutterstock.com.
Page 7: Jarno Gonzalez Zarraonandia/
Shutterstock.com.
Page 8: Jarno Gonzalez Zarraonandia/
Shutterstock.com.

Duotones
Page 30: Naoki Kakuta/Shutterstock.com.
Page 58: Alberto Loyo/Shutterstock.com.

Printed in India by Replika Press Pvt Ltd

Publishing information

Footprint Bilbao & Basque Region
4th edition
© Footprint Handbooks Ltd
April 2017

ISBN: 978 1 911082 17 0
CIP DATA: A catalogue record for this book
is available from the British Library

® Footprint Handbooks and the
Footprint mark are a registered
trademark of Footprint Handbooks Ltd

Published by Footprint
5 Riverside Court
Lower Bristol Road
Bath BA2 3DZ, UK
T +44 (0)1225 469141
footprinttravelguides.com

Distributed in the USA by
National Book Network, Inc.

Every effort has been made to ensure that
the facts in this guidebook are accurate.
However, travellers should still obtain advice
from consulates, airlines, etc about travel
and visa requirements before travelling.
The authors and publishers cannot
accept responsibility for any loss, injury
or inconvenience however caused.